PRAISE FOR *IT'S NOT OVER*

"I grew up in Massachusetts, and seeing the wild, wonderful adventure Josh is on there made it so easy to endorse this book. If you've ever thought it's too late to make an impact with your life or that you don't have the right set of skills or strengths, read this book. There's real hope inside and, maybe even more important, there are real steps you can start taking today."

—JON ACUFF
NEW YORK TIMES BESTSELLING AUTHOR OF *FINISH: GIVE YOURSELF THE GIFT OF DONE*

"Pastor Josh Gagnon's faith and passion are contagious. His new book *It's Not Over* is practical, engaging, and power-packed with spiritual encouragement. Whether you are overcoming a disappointment or simply dreaming big, this book will build your faith and inspire you to do more than you thought possible."

—CRAIG GROESCHEL
PASTOR OF LIFE.CHURCH AND
NEW YORK TIMES BESTSELLING AUTHOR

"Josh Gagnon is a dreamer—but not just any dreamer. He's a dreamer who is brave enough and bold enough to accomplish those dreams through the power of the Holy Spirit and the persistence to see them through. Josh has a unique ability to encourage you to dream big while also preparing you for the realities required to bring a dream to life. If there is a God-given dream on your heart, *It's Not Over* is for you."

—JENNI CATRON
FOUNDER OF THE 4SIGHT GROUP AND AUTHOR OF
THE 4 DIMENSIONS OF EXTRAORDINARY LEADERSHIP

"Joshua Gagnon is a fresh and timely voice in the church. He's built an incredible, life-giving, and growing church in one of the most difficult places to do so (New England), all while creating healthy culture and leading with excellence. Don't hesitate for a second to partner with him to bring this book and many others to the public square. All of us need a road map and reminder to keep dreaming big, God-sized dreams. That's Joshua. He's the right voice, right now, to bring this book to life. Our culture is starving for hope and a fresh vision for life."

—BRAD LOMENICK
FOUNDER OF BLINC AND AUTHOR OF
H3 LEADERSHIP AND *THE CATALYST LEADER*

"There's a good chance that at one time, you thought so much was possible. Life has a way of popping that balloon. People tell you your dream won't work. Reality hits. And you just get . . . discouraged.

"I'm so grateful for Josh Gagnon's voice. Not only can you defy the critics, but you can crush the negative voices in your head that tell you that you can't. Josh has lived the last decade defying the odds in the name of Jesus. It's my hope you'll discover how you can too. Josh is a leader's leader, and his voice is a voice this generation needs to hear."

—CAREY NIEUWHOF
AUTHOR AND FOUNDING PASTOR OF CONNEXUS CHURCH

"What a special reminder of understanding God-sized dreams and how to recognize what they look like in your life, right where you are at. This book will help awaken the desires God has tucked in our hearts and call them out to life."

—JENNIE LUSKO
PASTOR (WITH LEVI LUSKO) OF FRESH LIFE CHURCH

"In *It's Not Over*, Joshua Gagnon has a unique message that we all need to hear: your dreams are not dead, and God isn't done with your life! As you read this book, you will find encouragement, hope, and renewed faith that God has a plan for your life."

—CHRIS HODGES
SENIOR PASTOR AT CHURCH OF THE HIGHLANDS AND
AUTHOR OF *THE DANIEL DILEMMA* AND *WHAT'S NEXT?*

"*It's Not Over* is an encouragement to everyone who is stuck in the past, wondering what could have been. Instead, look to the future and dare to imagine what God can do. Pastor Josh offers a reminder we so desperately need to hear: God isn't done working in our lives, and that is a very good thing."

—GREG SURRATT

FOUNDING PASTOR OF SEACOAST CHURCH AND PRESIDENT OF ARC

"Everyone has a dream. For some, it's nothing more than a lofty aspiration. But for others, the pursuit of a God-sized dream leads to an amazing and beautiful reality. In *It's Not Over*, you'll discover the difference between mere wishful thinking and the pursuit of a God-given dream as Josh Gagnon explores the predictable resistance and obstacles that every God-sized dream faces—and what it takes to keep toward the destination God has placed in your heart. Whether you feel like your dream is just now in the formative stage, has been shattered beyond repair, or is simply stalled out and going nowhere, you'll find great help and wisdom in these pages."

—LARRY OSBORNE

PASTOR OF NORTH COAST CHURCH AND AUTHOR

"In *It's Not Over*, Josh not only gives us permission to dare to dream big dreams again but also blazes a trail and demonstrates how. He shows us that it is no longer time to allow our fears, our failures, and our flaws debilitate us from the futures God has for us. If you let it, this book can change the trajectory of your life and the lives of those around you."

—LEVI LUSKO

PASTOR OF FRESH LIFE CHURCH AND BESTSELLING AUTHOR

"Pastor Gagnon gives us gentle reminders that as we go for our dreams, it is our faith that will keep us moving past the darkest moments. Without faith, we will not have hope, and without hope, we will not persevere. Always believe and never give up! *It's Not Over* will inspire you to keep going, focus on the positive, and overcome the odds."

—RUDY RUETTIGER

MOTIVATIONAL SPEAKER, AUTHOR, AND

INSPIRATION BEHIND THE FILM *RUDY*

IT'S NOT OVER

*Leaving Behind Disappointment
and Learning to Dream Again*

JOSHUA GAGNON

W PUBLISHING GROUP

AN IMPRINT OF THOMAS NELSON

Published in Nashville, Tennessee, by W Publishing, an imprint of Thomas Nelson. Published in association with The Bindery Agency, www.TheBinderyAgency.com.

Thomas Nelson titles may be purchased in bulk for educational, business, fund-raising, or sales promotional use. For information, please e-mail SpecialMarkets@ThomasNelson.com.

Unless otherwise noted, Scripture quotations are taken from the Holy Bible, New Living Translation. © 1996, 2004, 2007, 2013, 2015 by Tyndale House Foundation. Used by permission of Tyndale House Publishers, Inc., Carol Stream, Illinois 60188. All rights reserved.

Scripture quotations marked NIV are from the Holy Bible, New International Version®, NIV®. Copyright © 1973, 1978, 1984, 2011 by Biblica, Inc.™ Used by permission of Zondervan. All rights reserved worldwide. www.zondervan.com. The "NIV" and "New International Version" are trademarks registered in the United States Patent and Trademark Office by Biblica, Inc.™

Any Internet addresses, phone numbers, or company or product information printed in this book are offered as a resource and are not intended in any way to be or to imply an endorsement by Thomas Nelson, nor does Thomas Nelson vouch for the existence, content, or services of these sites, phone numbers, companies, or products beyond the life of this book.

ISBN 978-0-7852-3065-6 (eBook)
ISBN 978-0-7852-3062-5 (TP)

Library of Congress Cataloging-in-Publication Data

Library of Congress Control Number: 2019952448

Printed in the United States of America

20 21 22 23 24   LSC   10 9 8 7 6 5 4 3 2 1

Jennifer, you are the most amazing woman I've ever known, and being able to call you my wife is proof that dreams come true. You are the purest example of a Jesus follower I've ever met, and I am a better me because I am with you. I love you always and forever.

Malachi and Nehemiah, never settle for a life of mediocrity. Instead, chase dreams that are God-sized. If I could line up all the boys in the whole world and only choose two, I would choose you every time. Words will always fall short of describing my love for you, but here's my best attempt: I love you.

CONTENTS

FOREWORD

The day I met Josh Gagnon for the first time was a normal, regular, routine kind of day—until it wasn't.

I was sitting in my office above Ebenezers, our coffeehouse on Capitol Hill. I don't remember what I was working on exactly, but it must have been something a little mundane. A little boring. Because I was glad when one of our staff members knocked on the door.

"There's a pastor downstairs who'd like to see you," she said. "You busy?"

"Who is it?" I asked.

She shrugged and shook her head. "No appointment."

That caught my attention. By then, National Community Church had been listed as one of the most innovative, most influential churches in America. So it wasn't unusual for pastors to reach out via email, via phone. But just dropping in unannounced? That was rare! Then the staff member said, "I think he's planting a church in New England."

That *really* caught my attention. Once a church planter, always a church planter. There are very few people I enjoy spending time with more than church planters. That's my tribe! Especially if they have the courage to plant a church in New England, one of the least churched corners of our country.

And so, before I even met him, I knew several important things about Josh Gagnon. I knew he had the faith to plant a church where few others have tried and even fewer have succeeded. I knew he had the courage to drive hundreds of miles and show up on my doorstep without any prior connection to me or even a phone call to make sure I was in town. And I knew he was the kind of person I wanted to learn more about.

Josh and I talked a lot that first day, mostly about our dreams. And what I liked about him from the very beginning is that he wasn't just dreaming big dreams—he was *chasing* them. He was hunting them down with a full confidence in God's power and a heartfelt desire to see God glorified.

Sadly, the pursuit of big dreams is a dying art in today's world. As I look around, there are fewer and fewer people willing to pray bold prayers and reach for God-sized goals.

This is even true within the church. Maybe it's true *especially* within the church. As disciples of Jesus and heirs to everything He accomplished and everything He promised, we so often settle for what feels safe. Efficient. Achievable. Realistic.

But let me ask you: What is the point of seeking God's presence and God's power to realize goals that are achievable without God's help? Why should we settle for what seems reasonable when we have access to divine provision? Divine empowerment?

Remember what the Scriptures say:

- "Now all glory to God, who is able, through his mighty power at work within us, to accomplish infinitely more than we might ask or think" (Eph. 3:20).

- "And this same God who takes care of me will supply all your needs from his glorious riches, which have been given to us in Christ Jesus" (Phil. 4:19).
- "By his divine power, God has given us everything we need for living a godly life. We have received all of this by coming to know him, the one who called us to himself by means of his marvelous glory and excellence. And because of his glory and excellence, he has given us great and precious promises. These are the promises that enable you to share his divine nature and escape the world's corruption caused by human desires" (2 Pet. 1:3–4).

For these reasons and more, I couldn't be more excited about *It's Not Over*. This is such a critical message for our day! We've all experienced disappointment. We've all had those moments where we stop, take a look around, and think, *How did I get here? What happened?*

But as Josh says, if there's still breath in our lungs, there's still time to chase the dreams God has planted inside us.

That's worth saying again: you still have time! You still have an incredible opportunity to be the person you've always known you can be. To make the impact you've always wanted to make. To chase the dream you've always wanted to chase and *take hold of it* for the glory of God.

So what are you waiting for?

In the years since our first meeting, I've watched Josh Gagnon chase after and realize many big dreams—what he rightly calls God-sized dreams. I've also had the privilege of supporting him along the way. Praying with him. Speaking at his church. Celebrating with him. To be frank, I've been blown away by the success of Next Level Church in New England, which is now the church home to thousands of people across many campuses.

What an incredible story!

It's funny: I used to think there was nothing Josh was more passionate about than pursuing his dreams. But now I'm not so sure. Because I've observed over the years that he gets incredibly excited and amazingly invested whenever he has the chance to help *others* pursue and achieve their God-sized dreams. He loves doing whatever it takes to help people dream again, and he's more than willing to offer his own sweat and tears to help others chase what they once believed to be impossible.

That's why he's written *It's Not Over*. Because he is passionate about your dreams. About your success. About you becoming the person God created you to be and achieving what He planted in your heart from the very beginning.

As you read this book, you can trust him to help you see where disappointment and discouragement have derailed the pursuit of your most precious dreams and your most treasured hopes for tomorrow. You can trust him to help guide you back on the right course with practical ideas and big-picture advice. And you can trust him to cheer you on every step of the way as you learn not only to dream again but to chase your God-sized dreams—and to keep chasing until you've got them.

I hope you will trust my friend Josh with all of that and more. Because he's right: it's not over!

—Mark Batterson

Lead pastor of National Community Church and *New York Times* bestselling author

INTRODUCTION

A Great, Big, Beautiful Tomorrow

All our dreams can come true, if we have the courage to
pursue them.

—WALT DISNEY[1]

"You know this is proof, right?"

I was at Disney World, speaking to my wife, Jennifer, as we
waited in line for one of the popular rides. I don't remember
which ride, but I do remember it was hot. And humid. And
crowded. And noisy.

"Oh, yeah?" Jennifer raised her eyebrows as she fanned
herself with a park map, trying to create a little breeze. "Proof
of what?"

Before I answered, I looked over at our sons, Malachi and
Nehemiah. They were reading through one of those informa-
tional placards they build into the waiting areas of Disney rides
in an attempt to make the lines less boring. Then I looked back
into my wife's eyes, smiled, and said, "Proof that I love you."

We both knew it was true. My love for my family is the *only* thing that motivates me to join them at zoos, fairs, stadiums—and especially at amusement parks. I once waited in line four hours just so my sons could meet Woody and Buzz Lightyear, their heroes from *Toy Story*. Now that's love!

These days, my boys no longer care about meeting larger-than-life characters. Instead, they've become adventure seekers, tackling the likes of Space Mountain, Rock 'n' Roller Coaster, and the Tower of Terror. Jennifer too. I'm not a fan of rides that go faster than five miles an hour, so I spend our days at Disney either sitting on the sidelines or going on what my sons call "old-people rides."

One of my favorite old-people rides is the Carousel of Progress, which is a rotating stage show that debuted at the 1964 World's Fair in New York. The carousel takes you on a simulated time-travel experience with animatronic characters from different periods of the twentieth century, each describing how technology has improved their lives.

One of the main features of that ride is a song called "There's a Great Big Beautiful Tomorrow," which gets repeated over and over again throughout the experience. The song describes a great big beautiful tomorrow that shines at the end of each day—a tomorrow that's a better version of today. A tomorrow we can access by following both our minds and our hearts.

According to the song, this great big beautiful tomorrow is only a dream away.

I've probably heard that song a hundred times by now, but I still enjoy it. I find the music calming and the lyrics inspiring.

Actually, *enjoy* might not be a strong enough word. The truth is, I get choked up every time I go on that ride. Even now, after all these years, I have to wipe away a few tears as I leave the theater. Yes, it's a bit awkward when I'm surrounded by a bunch of little kids and I look as if I've just finished watching the movie *Titanic*, but I can't help it. It makes me emotional.

The reason that ride affects me so much is because it's all about the power dreams have to shape our lives—to influence both who we are and what we can become.

As you get to know me throughout this book, you'll see that I'm passionate about dreams. In fact, I believe that pursuing a dream is essential to living a life with purpose. It's as vital to life as eating is to nourishment and breathing is to consciousness. This is especially true of God-sized dreams, which are those burning desires we often bury deep in our hearts because it seems as if there's *no way* we can accomplish them—at least, not through our own wisdom and strength.

I know firsthand how amazing it feels to achieve that kind of dream. It's life-changing in so many ways! But I also know what it's like to carry the disappointment and despair of watching a treasured dream slowly wither over time and feeling as though there's nothing you can do to stop it from dying completely.

But here's the good news: nobody needs to keep carrying that disappointment or continue living in that despair. There's a better way.

A DREAM COME TRUE

Years ago, I had a dream of starting a church. Specifically, I wanted to launch a church for people who didn't enjoy or feel comfortable in what we think of as a "traditional" church experience. I wanted to be part of a community where people didn't have to pretend all the time—where we could be real.

Growing up, and even into adulthood, I attended churches that often failed to deal with the issues that were important to regular people. I noticed that my friends associated the church with holding picket signs rather than sharing the love of Jesus. And as I looked around, it felt as if many of the Christians I knew cared more about what folks wore to church and whether they had the right opinions than about being real and allowing Jesus to meet them where they were.

I wanted to see a church that was relevant and life-giving. A place that made sense in today's culture—one that actually loved the community around it. A place that helped people experience life and joy and peace instead of guilt and disappointment.

Basically, I wanted a place where I could serve Jesus and still be myself.

In 2008, my wife and I officially launched Next Level Church in Dover, New Hampshire. We had no money. We had no congregation. And we had no experience as church planters. At that time, we didn't even realize we were trying to plant a church in the least churched region of the United States.

All we had was the dream.

Today, Next Level Church is one of the fastest-growing congregations in the world, with nine locations spread across several different states. I don't say that because I'm prideful about the growth or because I want you to think of me as a success. No, I say that because I'm so excited that my dream is coming true! There have been many obstacles along the way—we still face some today—and there have definitely been times when I've felt as if everything were about to come crashing down. And yet, each day when I go to work, I feel like a kid on Christmas morning who somehow got exactly what he wanted with every single gift.

It's an incredible feeling, and it's one I want to share. In fact, one of my primary goals as a pastor is leading the members of my community to not only identify their God-sized dreams but also take action toward achieving them. Along the same lines, I love getting the chance to speak with those who are longing so desperately to break free from the disappointments of yesterday and take hold of the hope found in tomorrow. Let me tell you, when I get the privilege of walking alongside people who finally—finally!—get to realize a dream or let go of a burden that's been dragging them down toward despair, it's an amazing experience.

Of course, within my role as a pastor, I also engage with many people on the other side of the fence. Meaning, as I interact with those in my community—and now even as I travel around the country and around the world—I regularly encounter people who have been carrying their disappointment for so long that they've lost the will to dream. These are people whose lives are devoid of hope. People who receive little or nothing from their dreams today and who expect nothing more from the future than a dark and discouraging tomorrow.

This isn't an attitude or a lifestyle that develops overnight. It takes a lot of time and a lot of disappointment. I see it in people who dreamed of getting married but have given up after years of looking for love and never finding it. I also see it in those who dreamed of having their marriages restored but gave up after a decade with no change. I see it in those who dreamed of victory over destructive habits but have settled into a crippling addiction after failing again and again. It's in those who have been believing God faithfully for an answer to prayer but are beginning to lose faith. And I see it in those who started life with a compelling vision of their purpose and what they would achieve but who are simply tired of constantly falling short.

And it's obvious that the world doesn't help. Society, with all its expectations, doesn't help. I know people who have been told again and again that their best days are behind them. That they're too old, that they've failed too often, and that they're not smart enough or spiritual enough or talented enough or _____ enough to achieve their dreams.

These are false narratives, and we often know them to be false—at first. But when we hear them over and over again and constantly feel the weight of dreams that have yet to be realized, those narratives begin to take root in our hearts.

If you can relate to any of these ideas, or if you're carrying the weight of disappointment even now, please keep reading. Because you really can learn to dream again. I'm living proof that it's possible!

DON'T SETTLE FOR MEDIOCRE

This book almost didn't happen, and it's not because I didn't want to write it. Actually, it's been a dream of mine to write for many years. No, this book almost didn't happen because I almost allowed disappointment to kill that dream. Almost.

Several years ago, I put together a book proposal and

went through the process of seeking a publisher. It was tough and terrifying, which I've now learned is common for most first-time authors. I had people who helped me, and they did everything possible to land me a book deal. But in the end, each of our leads dried up.

One of the publishers actually included a personal note in the rejection letter that said, "Josh isn't a gifted writer."

I'll be honest: that was a punch to the gut. It hurt. And because it hurt, I closed the door on my dream of writing a book. In fact, the morning after I received that letter, I told God during a time of prayer that I was giving up—that I would never write a book. I also expressed how angry and upset I was that He had closed the door so completely on a dream I thought had come from Him.

In the months that followed, several people asked me about writing. That's common when you lead a church that grows beyond a certain size. But every time someone mentioned the idea, I changed the subject. I wouldn't even consider it. As far as I was concerned, the dream was dead.

Then, almost a year to the day I had received that note from a publisher, a literary agent contacted me out of the blue. He said I'd been recommended by several people he trusted, and after researching me and listening to several of my sermons, he wanted to know if I had any interest in writing a book.

You know what I did? Nothing. I didn't even respond.

Looking back, I think I was aware that my dream wasn't dead but merely sleeping. Yet, because of the pain and disappointment I still carried, I didn't want to wake it up. Rejection is a painful thing. So I told myself, *I'm not a gifted writer,* and I tried to ignore what God was doing.

But that's the thing about God-sized dreams: they don't give up. They keep burning, even when we do everything in our power to stuff them down and snuff the flame to ashes. I couldn't ignore the idea that this book really could be a blessing to people—that what I had to share could help people let go of disappointment and start dreaming and living a life of hope again.

Almost a full year after I heard from that agent, I finally wrote him back. "I can't shake this passion inside me," I said. "I want to give it another try."

> THAT'S THE THING ABOUT GOD-SIZED DREAMS: THEY DON'T GIVE UP.

The fact that you are reading these pages tells you the end of the story. But as you continue to read, I hope you'll remember that I understand the weight of disappointment. I know what it's like to feel crushed by dreams that never seem to come true. I know what it feels like to be rejected, to feel inadequate, and to begin praying small, safe prayers because big, bold ones often carry the risk of large disappointment.

At the same time, I've learned again and again that even when it feels like it's over, it's not over!

What about you? I don't know your story, but I bet there was a time when you had dreams that took your breath away. You prayed they would come true, chased after them relentlessly, and turned over every rock that stood in the way. Is that dream still alive? Is it sleeping? Or have you settled for a simplified version of what you once desired?

Whatever your situation, it's not too late. There's still time to break free from the mundane and the mediocre. You don't have to live in the shadows of yesterday. You don't have to keep carrying the pain of your failures. You don't have to settle for safe prayers that take little or no faith. No! You still have a chance to chase after your God-sized dreams and your God-given future. And I would love the privilege of walking alongside you as you get started.

To accomplish that, we'll start by gaining a firm understanding of what God-sized dreams are and how to recognize them in our lives. Next, we'll take a head-on look at the obstacles that often derail our dreams, including disappointment, discontentment, and resistance from outside sources. Finally, we'll walk through several ways—both practical and spiritual—to overcome those obstacles and start dreaming again.

As we work through these pages together, I believe God will revive dead goals, breathe new life into dormant hopes, and birth brand-new dreams—for you and for me.

PURSUING

A DREAM IS

ESSENTIAL TO

LIVING A LIFE

WITH PURPOSE.

one

SWEET DREAMS ARE MADE OF THIS

> There is no use in running before you are sent; there
> is no use in attempting to do God's work without God's
> power. A man working without this unction, a man work-
> ing without this anointing, a man working without the
> Holy Ghost upon him, is losing time after all.
>
> —D. L. MOODY[1]

I happen to be a sucker for KFC commercials. I don't know
why, but when I see slow-motion images of that crispy, juicy,
golden-brown chicken piled high in those red-and-white
buckets, and then those flaky biscuits with the thick country
gravy, I have to remember to close my mouth to make sure I'm
not drooling.

Maybe you're too healthy to be a fried-chicken fan. If that's
the case, I don't understand you, and I'm a little sad for you

and jealous of you at the same time. But you still might be interested to know that KFC is the culmination of a lifelong dream—one that almost died before it even really got started.

Harland Sanders was born in 1890 and grew up on an Indiana farm. His father passed away when he was six years old, which meant Harland's mother had to go to work at a local canning factory to support her family. It also meant Harland himself became the primary caretaker for his younger siblings—which included cooking the family meals.

After leaving home, Sanders went on a bit of a journey to find himself. He worked as a streetcar conductor, served in the army, worked as a fireman for railroad companies, studied and practiced law, sold insurance, manufactured acetylene-lighting systems for farmers, sold tires, and more. In the middle of all that, he got married and had three children.

Motivating Sanders through each turn in his career path was a burning desire to provide a legacy for his family. Always a bit of a showman, he wanted to accomplish something big. Something memorable.

Finally, Sanders settled down in a little town called Corbin, Kentucky, where he ran a combination hotel and service station. To make some extra money, he started offering meals to weary travelers—home-cooked food for those who were tired of eating at greasy spoons. And wouldn't you know, they loved it! In fact, they couldn't get enough of it. Word spread up and down the highway that Sanders's food was too good to pass up. Soon, Sanders abandoned the service station entirely and instead built a restaurant, which could seat 142 people.

And then disaster struck. After ten years of increasing success, the government constructed a new interstate that completely bypassed Corbin, Kentucky—which meant there were no more customers for Harland Sanders. Dejected, he auctioned off the restaurant and its property in 1956. The sale price barely covered his debts and left him with little money and even less hope for the future.[2]

That's the moment when Sanders could have given up. That's the moment when his dream was closest to dying. After all, he was sixty-six years old and broke. What hope did he have for doing something big? Something memorable? Something to provide a legacy for his family?

In my experience, that's the moment when dreams die for so many people. When a crisis hits, when they don't understand how they can possibly move forward, most people respond by giving up. Or they settle for something smaller—something easier. And their dreams are buried in what-ifs and thoughts of what might have been.

Fortunately for fried-chicken fans everywhere, that's not how Harland Sanders responded. He was certain of one thing: he could make finger-lickin' good fried chicken. So he jumped into his 1946 Ford and hit the road.

Starting in Salt Lake City, Utah, Sanders began making deals with restaurant owners. His sales pitch was simple: if they gave him a nickel for every piece of fried chicken they sold, he would teach them how to prepare his secret recipe of eleven herbs and spices. He even spent days at each restaurant (and nights in the back of his car) preparing food for customers and showing chefs how to cook it perfectly every time. Sanders also required each restaurant that sold his chicken to display a large sign with his copyrighted logo and these words: FEATURING COLONEL SANDERS' RECIPE KENTUCKY FRIED CHICKEN.

By 1963, there were over six hundred restaurants that sold Sanders's chicken and displayed his sign. In 1964, he sold the business for $2 million, and he negotiated a further salary of $250,000 per year to serve as the primary face and spokesman for Kentucky Fried Chicken until the end of his life.[3]

How's that for a dream come true?

DEFINING A GOD-SIZED DREAM

Maybe right now you're thinking, *You're a pastor, so aren't you supposed to talk about spiritual things? And isn't this book supposed to help me pursue the kinds of dreams that will help me find fulfillment and purpose in my life? Why are you talking about fried chicken?*

Good questions. The answer to the first question is that Harland Sanders was both a fried-chicken entrepreneur *and* a follower of God. In fact, he was made an honorary colonel by the governor of Kentucky in 1935 because of his humanitarian work and community service—that's how he became "Colonel Sanders"!

The answer to the second question is that Colonel Sanders did live a life of purpose and fulfillment. He was a simple man at heart, who spent little and donated the vast majority of his fortune to charities, including helping to found and support several children's hospitals. Meaning, his dream of crafting and selling the world's best fried chicken has literally saved lives. Even now, decades after the Colonel passed away, his pursuit of that dream is still saving lives.

Think about that the next time you gobble down some KFC! (Or a salad at the restaurant next door.)

All joking aside, the main reason I'm sharing these details is because Colonel Sanders's story is a great illustration of what I often refer to as a "God-sized dream."

To put it simply, a God-sized dream is a compelling vision, goal, or longing that drives us toward something way too big for us to accomplish on our own. It's a dream or a yearning we feel inside—usually it's something that we deeply desire to achieve or experience—and yet we often have no idea how to bring it about.

That word *compelling* is important. God-sized dreams are those desires inside us that simply won't be ignored. When we pay attention to them and spend time pursuing them, we feel exhilarated. We feel joy and purpose—as though we're doing exactly what we were created to do. On the other hand, when we try to ignore our God-sized dreams or move away from them, it burns. It's like indigestion of the soul.

> A GOD-SIZED DREAM IS A COMPELLING VISION, GOAL, OR LONGING THAT DRIVES US TOWARD SOMETHING WAY TOO BIG FOR US TO ACCOMPLISH ON OUR OWN.

For example, I mentioned in the introduction that I caught a vision as a young man to plant a church. More specifically, I wanted to plant a successful church that would serve the needs of people in a real way but would also look and feel different from what I had experienced in churches for most of my life. I wanted to build a new kind of community, and I wanted to build it in a place where people generally don't go to church.

That was my God-sized dream, and for years I went back and forth between trying to ignore it and trying to make it happen. I tried to talk myself out of it. I would remind myself of all the reasons it didn't make any sense for me to be a pastor, let alone plant a church: I didn't have the right education, I didn't have any experience, and I'd never been the kind of guy that people looked at and thought, *He's going to do great things for Jesus.*

None of it worked. I wanted to run away from the dream of planting a church so many times, but each time I tried, it kept pulling me back in.

Looking back, I can remember specific times when I chose to ignore the list of reasons and excuses as to why my dream would never become a reality—and in those moments, I always felt so alive! I remember preaching sermons to myself as I drove down the road in my 1998 Ford Bronco. That gas-guzzler was my first pulpit. It's where I first learned to speak from my heart and listen for the quiet voice of the Holy Spirit. It's where I first became burdened for my friends who were far from God. (I think I even led myself to Jesus during one of my steering-wheel altar calls!)

Back in those days, it was just God and me, driving down the road. It was an unforgettable period of my life, and those memories are precious to me. Now I understand that the joy I experienced was a sure and certain sign that I was pursuing a God-sized dream, even though I didn't always recognize it at the time.

Of course, I still had no idea how to start a church—which

is another element that's often true of God-sized dreams: they are beyond us. They typically involve goals or visions that we simply cannot achieve on our own. And that's why we might try to hide them or push them down, because we know we're inadequate to achieve what we so deeply desire, and the awareness of that inadequacy can become painful if we don't use it to turn toward God.

That's a major problem today. So many people have rejected living out their God-sized dreams because they are focused on who *they* are instead of who *God* is. When we remember that God's strength begins where our strength ends, we'll have the freedom to chase after dreams we once thought were impossibilities.

That being the case, I'm thankful God knew exactly what He was doing when He planted that dream inside me to start a church. And I'm thankful I eventually stopped trying to figure things out on my own and chose to allow *Him* to accomplish *His* dream through me.

Don't miss that truth: God-sized dreams come from God. I know that sounds obvious, but it's an important distinction. When I conceive of a dream in my own mind and heart, I can easily squash it if I choose to do so. Because the dream or the goal has its source inside me, I can choose to let it go and stop thinking about it.

God-sized dreams are different because they have their source in God. That makes them harder to ignore. Harder to push aside. Even when we want to forget about them, they keep smoldering in our hearts.

I often share that one of the main reasons I continued to pursue my dream of planting Next Level Church in spite of all the obstacles and difficulties we encountered is that I knew abandoning that dream would mean disobeying God. There were times I tried to let the dream die, and there were plenty of times when people around me tried to convince me I had no business planting a church. (I'll share more about that later in the book.) But in the end, I couldn't let it go. I was aware that the Creator of the universe had placed this dream inside me, and that awareness kept driving me forward.

That's a God-sized dream.

One last thought: the kind of dream I'm talking about doesn't have to include a specific achievement or goal. A God-sized dream can be much broader, much simpler.

For example, one of my biggest dreams for a long time was simply to find security in my identity and in who Jesus made me to be. For many of my developing years, I always felt this huge sense of inadequacy—I carried a burden of believing I wasn't good enough and that I needed to accomplish something huge in order to feel loved or accepted by others. I longed for the day when I wouldn't feel as though I needed to prove myself.

In a similar way, your God-sized dream may simply be to find hope for the future. To overcome the pain and discouragement of the past. To feel stable or content or at peace. That's okay. In fact, I know from experience that those are amazing dreams to pursue!

CHARACTERISTICS OF A GOD-SIZED DREAM

Based on what we've explored so far, you may already have a sense of the God-sized dream or dreams that have been planted in your heart. You may even know exactly what dreams or goals fit into that category: your desire for a spouse, your prayer for a miracle, your longing for children, your goal to start a business, your hope for serving in a specific ministry, your desire for a certain career, your determination to overcome an addiction, and so on.

But I've also found that people can have a lot of confusion about what qualifies as a God-sized dream. After all, we have a lot of desires. It's natural for us to make goals and hope for achievements in different areas. So how do we determine whether a specific dream comes from God or is simply the result of that pizza or KFC we ate before bed last night?

I'd like to answer those questions by introducing one of the Bible's biggest dreamers: Nehemiah. This is one of my favorite Bible moments—in fact, I love it so much I named one of my sons Nehemiah! As we engage with his story, we'll find several characteristics that are often connected with God-sized dreams.

The Old Testament describes how God's people, the Israelites, repeatedly failed to follow Him, instead choosing to worship idols and false gods from other cultures. As a result, God sought new ways to get their attention and repeatedly gave them opportunities to turn back to Him.

Eventually, God implemented some tough love. Around 600 BC, God chose King Nebuchadnezzar and the Babylonians as His instrument to deliver a resounding message to His people. The Babylonian army invaded Israelite territory in three separate waves over a period of about twenty years. The third wave was the worst as the Babylonians killed countless Israelites, demolished their sacred temple in Jerusalem, and exported thousands of Israelites as slaves back to Babylon. When the invasion was over, Judah had been reduced to ruins, its people broken and scattered.

Nehemiah's ancestors were likely taken into captivity during the first wave of the Babylonian invasion. Meaning, Nehemiah was born to exiled parents.

With that background in place, let's take a deeper look at his story.

God-Sized Dreams Begin with a Need

Here's how Nehemiah introduced himself in Scripture, writing in the first person:

> In late autumn, in the month of Kislev, in the twentieth year of King Artaxerxes' reign, I was at the fortress of Susa. Hanani, one of my brothers, came to visit me with some other men who had just arrived from Judah. I asked them about the Jews who had returned there from captivity and about how things were going in Jerusalem. They said to me, "Things are not going well for those who returned to the province of Judah. They are in great trouble and disgrace. The wall of Jerusalem has been torn down, and the gates have been destroyed by fire." (Neh. 1:1–3)

It's important to remember that Nehemiah was born in exile, which means he had never seen Jerusalem—but he had surely heard about it. I can imagine the Israelite parents telling their children stories of the towering temple, the beautiful countryside, and the abundance of crops. This was their promised land, after all, the stuff of legends. Nehemiah would've grown up listening to tales of how God miraculously led His people into Jerusalem, of great battles and enemy defeats, and, even more importantly, of God's promise that His people would someday rebuild the temple and occupy Jerusalem again.

Now, imagine the horror and pain in Nehemiah's heart when he heard that the walls and gates of Jerusalem had been destroyed. In the ancient world, a city's walls were its primary means of defense against outside invaders, which meant Jerusalem was basically defenseless and in no condition for rebuilding.

The report from Judah broke something inside Nehemiah. That was the moment he thought, *This is not okay. Something has to be done!* Until that point, Nehemiah had been unaware of the state of Jerusalem's walls, but those words from his brother were the seed God used to spark in his heart the dream of rebuilding.

In a similar way, God-sized dreams are often planted in our hearts when we encounter a specific need. For some people, the sight of a hungry child immediately sparks a fire inside their hearts. For others, the thought of someone being homeless moves them deeply. Maybe the need that moves you is racial injustice, young people walking away from the church, current political issues, sex trafficking, Bible illiteracy, war, cancer, or any of a million other things.

It's also possible for personal longings to become the seed for God-sized dreams: the desire to get married, to witness a miraculous healing, to see your family restored, to launch a business, to break free from addiction, to develop self-confidence, and so on. There are moments when we hear about the devastation around us and we are driven to dream.

But there are also moments when dreams are birthed by the devastation within us.

In short, when God breaks your heart over a specific need, it's often the first sign that God is planting a dream inside you.

As I mentioned earlier, my own dream to launch Next Level Church was sparked by my desire to find a church community I could feel comfortable in—one where I could fit in without feeling as if I had to pretend I was someone else. Later, as the dream developed, I also realized there was a deep need for just such a community in the relatively unchurched area of New England, and now God is enlarging the dream to other regions of the country.

God-Sized Dreams Create Open Doors

While God-sized dreams often begin with our response to a specific need, there are lots of needs in our world. Actually, there are lots of needs in each of our communities. So we need more input when it comes to identifying which needs (and which dreams) God is using to direct our steps.

I like the way Nehemiah responded after his heart was broken by the Jerusalem report: "When I heard this, I sat down and wept. In fact, for days I mourned, fasted, and prayed to the God of heaven" (Neh. 1:4). Notice that Nehemiah didn't rush into action. Instead, he stopped and sought direction from God through prayer and fasting.

In other words, he waited for God to open a door. He waited to see what God was doing and how he could get on board.

And when that door eventually opened, it opened in a huge way:

Early the following spring, in the month of Nisan, during the twentieth year of King Artaxerxes' reign, I was serving the king his wine. I had never before appeared sad in his presence. So the king asked me, "Why are you looking so sad? You don't look sick to me. You must be deeply troubled."

Then I was terrified, but I replied, "Long live the king! How can I not be sad? For the city where my ancestors are buried is in ruins, and the gates have been destroyed by fire."

The king asked, "Well, how can I help you?"

With a prayer to the God of heaven, I replied, "If it please the king, and if you are pleased with me, your servant, send me to Judah to rebuild the city where my ancestors are buried." (2:1–5)

The king himself asked Nehemiah how he could help him accomplish his dream! How cool is that? Nehemiah didn't have to knock down doors or try to position himself in God's favor. He stayed faithfully planted where God had placed him, and then God brought the opportunity to him.

As modern people with a "go get 'em" mentality, we spend so much time trying to manipulate our way into greater opportunities. We are often desperate to make things happen. But in a split second, God can open doors that we've spent years trying to crack. Remember this: you don't have to force your way into God's plan; you just need to move in His direction when He opens a door.

I don't know what door God will open to point you toward your dreams, but you'd better be paying attention when He moves. Imagine if Nehemiah had missed the chance to tell the king what had been stirring within him. *Well, this isn't really an appropriate subject for work . . .* Instead, Nehemiah pounced, and so should we.

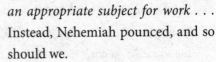

YOU DON'T HAVE TO FORCE YOUR WAY INTO GOD'S PLAN; YOU JUST NEED TO MOVE IN HIS DIRECTION WHEN HE OPENS A DOOR.

Your open door could be a chance encounter with the CEO of the company where you always dreamed of working. Maybe that great guy you see on the subway each day really is worth your time. Maybe it's that college-acceptance letter you received, even though you don't yet know how you'll pay the tuition. Or maybe it's an opportunity to be mentored by someone who can help you find security in your God-given identity, or to go on a mission trip through your church.

You might be thinking, *But how do I know which opportunities are God opening a door and which are just happenstance? How do I know when to jump?*

Remember what Nehemiah did: as soon as his heart was broken for Jerusalem, he prayed and fasted. Meaning, he turned to God and stayed close to Him. He sought God's direction rather than trying to make his own path, and, therefore, he was ready when God opened the door. The same can be true for us when we stay close to God each day and seek direction from His Holy Spirit.

When it comes to finding God's will for your life, your heart matters more than your decisions. What I mean is that God is not up in heaven playing a big game of "pick the correct door." Many people go through life afraid of making decisions—afraid that if they choose wrong, they'll ruin their lives. This results in stagnation. Such people want to move, but their feet are stuck in the quicksand of what-ifs.

I love these words from Proverbs 3:5–6: "Trust in the LORD with all your heart and lean not on your own understanding; in all your ways submit to him, and he will make your paths straight" (NIV). Remember this: our God is a good Father, and He's able to *make* our paths straight even if we start down the wrong path.

If we are diligent in seeking God with all our hearts, He is able to bring us where we need to be even when we choose the wrong door—and He's promised He will do it. We don't have to be paralyzed by the fear of wrong decisions; we can live in freedom, knowing that if we seek God as Nehemiah did, He is more than capable of straightening our paths.

You may be asking, *So I can just do whatever I want and God will make my path straight?* Not quite. Remember, God straightens the paths of those who are seeking Him. By definition, we cannot seek His will and "do whatever we want" at the same time. When we seek His will and line up our lives with His desires, God will make our paths straight, because He has always cared more about our hearts than our decisions.

My "choose a path" moment came when I was working as a youth pastor, preaching every Wednesday night to students and also to nursing-home residents. One day when I was teaching at a youth conference, I met a small group of people from a church that had recently shut down; they no longer had a pastor. They were older saints, and I respected them—still do. They told me they saw the hand of God over my life, and they asked if I had ever thought about starting a church.

This may sound silly, but until that moment, I had never really considered how churches got started. I had dreamed of being a pastor, but I had no idea what that would look like or what it would take to *start* a church. So I laughed off their suggestion. Yet even in that moment, there was something inside me that jumped at the thought. Pretty soon, I couldn't think of much else. The dream was that strong!

When I later found ten friends who agreed to be part of the launch team with Jen and me, we jumped. And we've been moving forward ever since.

A God-sized dream requires a God-sized opportunity; it also requires the willingness to seek God first and *then* to make a decision. So be patient, be watchful, seek after Him, and be ready to leap through that door when it opens.

God-Sized Dreams Match Our Abilities and Experience

Let's look back to Nehemiah's story and see what happened after he finally arrived in Jerusalem:

> So I arrived in Jerusalem. Three days later, I slipped out during the night, taking only a few others with me. . . .
>
> The city officials did not know I had been out there or what I was doing, for I had not yet said anything to anyone about my plans. I had not yet spoken to the Jewish leaders—the priests, the nobles, the officials, or anyone else in the administration. But now I said to them, "You know very well what trouble we are in. Jerusalem lies in ruins, and its gates have been destroyed by fire. Let us rebuild the

wall of Jerusalem and end this disgrace!" Then I told them about how the gracious hand of God had been on me, and about my conversation with the king.

They replied at once, "Yes, let's rebuild the wall!" So they began the good work. (Neh. 2:11–12, 16–18)

In the book of Nehemiah, his leadership stands out. You can see it in these verses as he secretly inspected the wall by night and then rallied the people of the city to join his cause. "Let us . . . end this disgrace!" By the time he finished his speech, all the people were champing at the bit to begin their "good work."

I'm not surprised at Nehemiah's leadership effectiveness because of where his story began. Do you remember what he was doing in Persia? He was the cupbearer to the king. That meant he sampled all the king's food and drink to check for poison, which obviously was an important job. That also meant Nehemiah was one of the king's key advisers. He was someone the king trusted.

Therefore, Nehemiah must have been a natural leader. Even as a foreigner, he was able to rise through the ranks and become a key administrator in the Persian kingdom.

When it came to rebuilding the walls around Jerusalem, Nehemiah obviously needed to recruit some help. He needed expert builders, skilled artisans, strong men to haul stones, guards to stand watch, and carpenters to build the gates and doors. Though all of this special talent was crucial, the dream required Nehemiah's unique leadership ability most of all. God assigned Nehemiah the critical role of leading the project, but He also uniquely equipped him with the leadership ability to achieve it.

In a similar way, God-sized dreams typically align well with our abilities and life experiences. That's why we often find fulfillment and purpose when we pursue those dreams—we are doing exactly what God uniquely created us to do.

So what are you good at? What comes easily to you? Are you good at working with your hands? Do you like math? Do you enjoy speaking in public? Are you a natural leader? Do you love to write? Do you enjoy initiating things? Do you love animals? Do you love kids? Do you enjoy teaching?

Don't overcomplicate it. God's will for your life will typically align with your divine giftedness. Ask yourself, *Is that what's happening in my life right now? In my career? In my ministry opportunities? Am I being given opportunities to use my greatest gifts?*

Now, I say "typically" because there are times when God may ask you to jump into something new. In my life, for example, I had no pastoral experience before we launched Next Level Church. No official training. There was a big learning curve for me. Looking back, however, I can say with confidence that God designed me to be a pastor. That includes how much I enjoy teaching, my love for people, and my ability to lead—all of those and more are part of who I am and who I've always been. It just took me a little while to realize it.

God made each person specifically and uniquely. Even identical twins have distinct interests, desires, and abilities. This is all by design. God chose a unique dream just for you and shaped you with the exact experiences, skills, and abilities you need to accomplish it. He does not intend for your unique talents to go to waste!

God-Sized Dreams Create Opposition

I hated elementary school for a lot of reasons, but one of the biggest (literally and figuratively) was a bully named Billy. Every day, from the moment I got on the bus to the moment I finally got back off, he picked on me. He would hit me, call me names, and try to embarrass me in every way imaginable. (Billy, if you're reading this, I'm still afraid of you!)

I finally told my mom about Billy one day after school. She was pretty upset, but I begged her not to say anything to the principal. Instinctively, I knew that would only make things worse. To my surprise, my mom agreed. In hindsight, I should have realized that was too easy.

The next day, Mom walked me to the bus as usual—but then she kept going. She went right through the doors, up the little stairs, and yelled out, "Who's Billy?"

Billy wasn't a dummy. He cowered down in his seat and didn't say a word. He didn't succeed in hiding, though, because the rest of the kids on the bus were all pointing at him in unison.

My mom marched up to his seat and spoke in a voice of cold fury. "If you are ever mean to Joshua again, you will have to deal with me!" Needless to say, I never had a problem with Billy or any other bullies in elementary school. Word got around.

I mention that story because I know, for many people, it's easy to think that when God plants a dream in your heart, it's smooth sailing from that moment on. Nope! That's not the case at all. In fact, pursuing a God-sized dream almost always involves a lot of obstacles and opposition. Why is that? Because evil really does exist in the world, and we really do have an Enemy—a bully worse than a thousand Billys—who is actively seeking to derail God's plan for our lives. This is especially true when it comes to chasing our God-given, God-inspired dreams.

Look at what Nehemiah experienced, for example:

> But when Sanballat and Tobiah and the Arabs, Ammonites, and Ashdodites heard that the work was going ahead and that the gaps in the wall of Jerusalem were being repaired, they were furious. They all made plans to come and fight against Jerusalem and throw us into confusion. But we prayed to our God and guarded the city day and night to protect ourselves. (Neh. 4:7–9)

Israel's enemies were not happy about the walls around Jerusalem being rebuilt. They preferred to keep Jerusalem a defenseless ruin, so they did everything they could to hinder and halt Nehemiah's work. In fact, throughout the book of Nehemiah, these same villains continue to pop up and throw monkey wrenches into Nehemiah's plans.

And it wasn't just Nehemiah. If you make a list of heroes in the Bible, you'll discover one common denominator they all share: opposition. Moses faced resistance countless times while wandering the desert for forty long years. Joseph's brothers sold him into slavery. David had to slay a giant and escape Saul's wrath. Paul was arrested, beaten, and shipwrecked. Most of the apostles were killed for their faith. And, oh yeah, let's not forget that Jesus was murdered by the very people He came to save!

Opposition is a prerequisite to achieving any great dream. Especially a God-sized dream. Don't be concerned when you are facing opposition; be concerned when your dreams are so small there is no reason for opposition.

We faced a lot of opposition during our efforts to launch and grow Next Level Church. For example, we had exactly $270 as our operating budget when we put together our first service. We also had no building, no property, and no congregation. However, the most destructive obstacles I had to overcome were my own sense of inadequacy and the criticism of other people who thought we had no chance of succeeding. (I'll talk about that a little more in chapter 4, which is about the resistance we face as we pursue our dreams.)

> DON'T BE CONCERNED WHEN YOU ARE FACING OPPOSITION; BE CONCERNED WHEN YOUR DREAMS ARE SO SMALL THERE IS NO REASON FOR OPPOSITION.

As I continue to work through opposition, one of the Scripture verses that encourages me the most is Psalm 3:3: "But you, O LORD, are a shield around me; you are my glory, the one who holds my head high."

When you face opposition, remember that God is your defender—but also remember that in order to be lifted up, you need to start low. Let me say it this way: God can't lift a head that isn't first bowed. We often make the mistake of trying to fight back and defend ourselves against opposition through our own wisdom and strength. That's a bad idea. Our best posture when staring in the face of obstacles is to bow in humility. God has promised to lift our heads high, so don't hinder His work by trying to elevate yourself.

WHAT'S YOUR GOD-SIZED DREAM?

Now it's your turn. Take a moment to think about your life and your dreams. What are the goals God has planted in your heart? What is a God-sized dream you have always wanted to pursue?

If you're having trouble pinning it down, think again through the characteristics we explored earlier:

- **Need:** What breaks your heart today? What are some needs in the world or in your community that always catch your attention? What are problems that prompt you to think, *Someone needs to do something about this*? That someone could be you!
- **Opportunity:** Where has God been opening doors in your life? What are some opportunities that made you feel excited—and if you didn't end up taking those opportunities in the past, could they still be there if you decided to jump?
- **Abilities and Experience:** What are some of the ways God has gifted you? What are some of the life experiences that have shaped you into the person you are today? You are a unique, talented individual whom God has uniquely designed to accomplish His will. (Note: if you have trouble thinking about your own talents, try talking with those who know you best. Ask them what they think you do really, really well.)
- **Opposition:** Have you started pursuing a dream but then gave it up because of all the obstacles thrown in your way? Maybe those obstacles were proof that you were on the right track! Think back over recent months and

identify those moments when it seemed as though your spiritual Enemy, circumstances, or opinions were pushing you away from a goal or desire. Perhaps that goal or desire was never meant to die.

If you know your God-sized dream, find a pen and write it down in the space below. Spill some ink! Make it official. What is your God-sized dream? What's a prayer you'll start believing again that God will answer? What hope or desire or promise have you dropped that you need to pick back up and start running with?

_____

_____

Keep this dream in mind as we work through the chapters to follow.

One final note: don't overthink things as you work to identify your God-sized dream(s). Just the other day, as my family and I were leaving our home to go out to dinner, I stopped and said, "Ah, I forgot my phone. Malachi, can you go grab it for me? I think it's in the kitchen."

Malachi ran off, eager to be the hero. But after a few minutes of looking, he came back and said, "Dad, I can't find it."

Confused, I started patting down my body, which is when I realized the phone had been in my back pocket the whole time. Have you ever done that? Actually, I've done worse. One time I started asking where my phone was, and then I noticed Jennifer pointing at it—in my hand!

Here's my point: in the same way I sometimes try to find a phone that isn't lost, we often try extra hard to discover dreams that aren't hiding. We sometimes ignore God-given dreams because they don't seem spiritual enough or important enough, or seem too simple and obvious. (Remember Colonel Sanders and his life-changing fried chicken?) Or worse, we fall into the trap of comparing our dreams with the dreams of others. For example, you might hear about a celebrity pastor with a dream and a mission to end world hunger, or a famous musician giving millions to charity—and then you start to feel embarrassed about the dream God planted in your heart to tutor kids who are struggling in school.

That's a natural response, but it's unhelpful. In fact, it's destructive.

Please hear me: you are responsible only for being faithful to the dreams God has called *you* to steward. Don't sit on the sidelines wondering where your dream is when, like Nehemiah, God has placed it right in front of you. No, you're not too old. No, you're not too young. You're not a collection of yesterday's mistakes, and you haven't used up your potential. You are God's masterpiece, and He has uniquely created you to accomplish your specific purpose.

Your great, big, beautiful tomorrow is just a God-sized dream away. It's right in front of you! But to find it, you may need to overcome some of the temptations that often cause us to stop dreaming.

GOD CHOSE A UNIQUE
DREAM JUST FOR YOU
AND SHAPED YOU WITH
THE EXACT EXPERIENCES,
SKILLS, AND ABILITIES YOU
NEED TO ACCOMPLISH IT.

two

LIFE ON A STUMP

The greatest glory in living lies not in never falling but in rising every time we fall.

—NELSON MANDELA[1]

"Dad! Come here!" I heard my son Malachi's voice, and he sounded excited. *I'm glad somebody's excited*, I thought. I was not at all overjoyed to be at the Tampa zoo in 105-degree weather with humidity and was once again proving my love for my family while the sun beat down on our skin and threatened to fry us like eggs.

Jennifer and the boys were zigzagging from exhibit to exhibit, apparently oblivious to the heat. I mentioned earlier that my undying affection for my wife and boys brings me to these parks, but in that moment the air-conditioning in my car was pushing hard for my attention.

"Dad, come on, quick!" my son's voice called again, and this time he piqued my curiosity when he added, "There's a bald eagle!"

Actually, as I trudged over to where he was standing, I saw two bald eagles, both relaxing in the sun. One was sitting high on a tree branch, while the other had settled on a stump. There was no net covering the habitat, so I wondered what was keeping those two wild birds from taking off. Then I read the small sign next to the exhibit: "The birds in this exhibit have sustained permanent injuries in the wild and cannot fly."

Of course, I thought. *You guys don't want to be here either.*

Ten feet from those beautiful birds, I just stared. These were fierce and feared kings of the sky—symbols of strength even back in ancient times, and icons today for everything I love about my country.

Did you know that a bald eagle can spread its seven-foot wingspan and soar up to ten thousand feet in the sky? The next time you're in an airplane, keep your window shade up during takeoff. Then, when the crew says, "We've reached ten thousand feet; you may now use your electronic devices," take a look outside. You'll see what an eagle sees. They soar through the sky at forty miles per hour, and they can spot their prey from over two miles away. And once it sees dinner, an eagle can nosedive for the kill at speeds up to one hundred miles per hour.

Eagles are at the top of the food chain for a reason!

In case you're wondering, I didn't know all of these eagle-related facts while l was standing there at ZooTampa—I looked them up later. But I did know that eagles were created to soar, not stand on a stump. And I couldn't help but wonder how they felt. *Do they miss the feeling of their beaks piercing the wind? Do they ever forget they've been injured and try to fly? Have they lost the desire to fly altogether? Do they stare at the sky all day and wonder,* What if?

As I stood next to my son and watched those magnificent birds who had once ruled the skies, I couldn't help thinking about the millions of people in this world who spend their lives waiting for a miracle—waiting for life to turn in the direction they always hoped it would go. Restaurants, schools, homes, and churches are filled with women and men who feel grounded by their pasts and live in a constant state of disappointment. These are people who genuinely want to end up somewhere different from where they currently are, yet they feel stuck. They're in a holding pattern.

Please hear me on this: you are capable of pursuing your dreams. As human beings, we've been uniquely fashioned and lovingly crafted in the image of our God, the Creator of the universe. Each one of us is designed for greatness. Each one of us has been created to soar!

That raises the question: Why don't we? Why do so many people settle for life on a stump? I think it's because they believe they're like those eagles, lacking the strength or the ability to soar. Maybe they used to believe they could fly, but no longer. Something happened that pulled them down to the ground, and now they don't have the faith or confidence to fly again.

This is something we all have to deal with at different times in our lives. We encounter obstacles and lies that—if we allow them to—convince us we're unable to soar. These obstacles are like weights that tether us to the ground and cause us to surrender our dreams. And the biggest and most common obstacle is disappointment.

THE ROOTS OF DISAPPOINTMENT

After years of teaching and talking about the need for people to let go of disappointment and learn to dream again, I've discovered that disappointment as a concept is pretty hard to define. When I use the word *disappointment*, it often means different things to different people because we experience disappointment on two different layers—one layer on the surface and another that goes much, much deeper.

The surface layer of disappointment is not really a big deal. For example, if I decide to keep saving lives by ordering a ten-piece bucket of Kentucky Fried Chicken, but then I get home and find I've been given only eight pieces, I'll be disappointed. I'll be a little miffed. I may even consider writing a strongly worded email. But the experience wouldn't stay with me. I'd probably forget about it entirely by the next day.

All of us experience disappointment in that way, and it happens regularly. It's just a part of life. But there's another layer of disappointment that is much more serious—a deeper layer. And that's the kind of disappointment we'll be focusing on in this chapter and throughout the rest of the book.

The dictionary defines *disappointment* as "the act or an instance of disappointing; the state or emotion of being disappointed." Not helpful, Webster! Thankfully, things get better when we dig a little deeper:

Disappointed: "defeated in expectation or hope"
Disappointing: "failing to meet expectations"[2]

Serious disappointment is a form of defeat. We want or need something, and we reach for it—but then we are thwarted. We're defeated in our efforts and defeated in our hopes. And it hurts.

But what really hurts is when we are defeated over and over again. And that's a key element in understanding this deeper layer of disappointment: it's ongoing. It's something we keep experiencing. And the more we experience it, the more it becomes part of who we are until, eventually, we develop a lifestyle of being defeated. A lifestyle of associating hope with hurt.

That's when we start to surrender not only our dreams but our ability to dream.

If you're single and you dream of being married, for example, then you don't feel defeated just once a year on Valentine's Day. Instead, you feel the sting every time a relationship ends. You feel it every time your mom drops another little hint about grandchildren. You feel it every time you hang out with married friends and everyone seems so happy and in love. Eventually, your hopes are defeated so many times that you try to let them go. You tell yourself the dream is dead, and you do your best to move on.

The Bible expresses these truths in a powerful way in Proverbs 13:12, which says, "Hope deferred makes the heart sick." Chances are good you've experienced that type of disappointment at some point in your life—that sickness of the heart. Maybe you're experiencing it now.

But here's an important question: What's at the root of our

experiences with serious, life-altering disappointment? What causes it?

Some people say that our hopes and desires are the root. They think that if we can just limit our dreams—if we can just be realistic about life—we'll eliminate the risk of getting hurt. But that's not easily done. Our hopes and desires are often planted in our hearts by God's design, and they serve a necessary role in spurring us on to pursue our dreams.

Others would say it's *unmet* hopes and desires that are the cause of serious disappointment, but that's not correct either. Think about it: you have many hopes and desires that have never been realized. So do I. When I was younger, I dreamed of playing in the NBA. I even had some skill on the basketball court—I played in college. Eventually, however, the fact that I'm a little under six feet tall helped me understand that my dream wasn't going to come true. It still hasn't come true to this day, but it's not a source of disappointment in my life; it's not a defeat that causes me pain or keeps me stuck.

The same is true for you. Right now, you have several hopes and desires that have not been realized. I'm sure every time you have a performance review at work, you hope to receive a promotion. I'm sure you desire many things for yourself and your loved ones that you have not yet received—a greater sense of peace, the ability to travel, more time with family, and so on—but the lack of what you desire doesn't make your heart sick.

So what *is* the root of serious disappointment in our lives? It's our unsurrendered expectations. By *expectations*, I mean those things we expect to happen in the near future—what we believe *should* happen. (Notice the word *expectations* appeared in both of the dictionary definitions highlighted earlier.)

Unsurrendered expectations are the expectations we pull close to our chest and refuse to let go. It's when we plan for something to happen and then expect God to get on board with our agenda. Worse, it's when we hold it against God when those plans fall through: "If You really loved me, God, You wouldn't have let me down in that way." "If You really heard my prayers, You would have answered them by now." "If You really were for me, God, my dreams would have come true a long time ago."

This is a critical point: we experience the kind of disappointment that undermines our ability to dream when the reality of our lives doesn't match up with our unsurrendered expectations. When we feel like we have earned or deserve what it is we are hoping, praying, and dreaming for, we are often left in despair when it doesn't happen.

That is what hurts.

When you believe you deserve that promotion and you expect it to happen, and then it goes to someone else—that's painful. When you believe you are supposed to be married and you expect God to bring that special person into your life any day now, any month now, any year now, and yet it never happens— that's what feels like a continual defeat. When you believe God is going to answer your prayer, and you pray persistently just as the Bible says, but then it doesn't happen how you expected

> WHEN WE FEEL LIKE WE HAVE EARNED OR DESERVE WHAT IT IS WE ARE HOPING, PRAYING, AND DREAMING FOR, WE ARE OFTEN LEFT IN DESPAIR WHEN IT DOESN'T HAPPEN.

and there doesn't seem to be anything changing in your life—that's what makes the heart sick.

Notice expectations can be both internal and external. In other words, it's common for us to develop our own expectations based on our own beliefs. Let me give you a few examples. We dream about finding victory over an addiction because we feel the struggle inside every day. That's an internal expectation. But we can also adopt expectations that are external—that come from other sources. Maybe all your friends have landed their dream jobs, and that increases your level of expectation for getting hired. Or maybe the culture you live in constantly pushes the idea that happiness is connected to stuff, so you build up an expectation that you'll finally be satisfied if you get that new phone or new car or dream house.

Unsurrendered expectations are dangerous. They are harmful because they produce disappointment, and over time that disappointment will sabotage your ability to recognize and pursue your God-sized dreams.

For the rest of the chapter, let's take a look at how these truths played out in the lives of two women who expected Jesus to do something huge on behalf of their family.

THE DEATH OF A DREAM

The book of John records the story of two sisters, Mary and Martha, who had a significant need. Their brother, Lazarus, was extremely ill, and in their minds there was only one way to solve the problem:

A man named Lazarus was sick. He lived in Bethany with his sisters, Mary and Martha. This is the Mary who later poured the expensive perfume on the Lord's feet and wiped them with her hair. Her brother, Lazarus, was sick. So the two sisters sent a message to Jesus telling him, "Lord, your dear friend is very sick." (John 11:1–3)

There are two important things to keep in mind about the context of this story. First, at this point in His public ministry, Jesus had already performed many of His most talked-about miracles, such as turning water into wine, casting out demons, and multiplying a few loaves of bread and some fish to feed five thousand people. Jesus had clearly displayed His supernatural power on several occasions, including His power to heal those who were sick.

Second, everyone in this family—Mary, Martha, and Lazarus—had been on the front lines of Jesus' ministry. All three were Jesus' friends, not just strangers in the crowd. They had seen His miracles firsthand, and they knew Him personally.

Because of those two truths, Mary and Martha thought, *We're close friends with Jesus, and He heals the sick. There's no reason for us to worry. Jesus will heal Lazarus just as He is healing everyone else.*

Here's what happened next:

But when Jesus heard about it he said, "Lazarus's sickness will not end in death. No, it happened for the glory of God so that the Son of God will receive glory from this." So although Jesus loved Martha, Mary, and Lazarus, he stayed where he was for the next two days. (John 11:4–6)

Once, when I was traveling to Florida to visit one of our Next Level Church locations, a TSA agent stopped me after I'd gone through the body-scanning machine. "Sir, what's in your pants?" he asked.

I didn't know how to answer that question, and frankly, I thought it was a bit rude.

He asked me again, "Sir, what's in your pants?"

Feeling beyond confused, I said, "Nothing. Nothing is in my pants!"

I could tell he was getting annoyed with me. He raised his voice and said, "What's that behind your knee?"

I had no idea what he was talking about.

"If you're not going to tell me, I'm going to have to find out," he said. "Larrryyyyyyyy!"

The next thing I knew, some TSA guy named Larry showed up, and I found myself with both officers in a small interrogation room. They stared at me as if I were a criminal, so I broke the awkwardness by asking the only question that came to mind: "Is this when I take down my pants?"

"Yeah, go ahead," Larry replied.

Nervously, I unbuckled my belt and lowered my pants just enough to reach my hand down to the back of my knee, which was the area where the scanner had indicated I was hiding something. As I reached down, I was shocked to feel that there *was* something there. I grabbed on to it and pulled out . . . a sock.

Apparently, I'd gotten dressed, eaten my breakfast, driven to the airport, and walked from the parking lot to the body scanner without realizing that a rogue sock was tucked behind my knee. It wasn't my fault I was completely unaware of the sock. My knowledge of the situation was limited to what I could see. I couldn't see the sock, so I didn't believe there was a sock. The X-ray machine pointed out something that was present but unseen.

In a similar way, Mary and Martha had a limited view of what was happening and what would happen with their brother. They couldn't see beyond their circumstances, but Jesus saw it all.

I can imagine Mary and Martha sitting next to Lazarus's bed, patting him on the hand. Maybe they whispered, "It's going to be okay. Jesus will come and make it all better." But I also imagine they kept looking over their shoulders. I'm sure every now and then one of them walked to the window and looked down the road for any sign of Jesus' arrival, feeling less and less hopeful with every passing minute.

When Jesus finally arrived, it was to a somber household:

> When Jesus arrived at Bethany, he was told that Lazarus had already been in his grave for four days. Bethany was only a few miles down the road from Jerusalem, and many of the people had come to console Martha and Mary in their loss. When Martha got word that Jesus was coming, she went to meet him. But Mary stayed in the house. Martha said to Jesus, "Lord, if only you had been here, my brother would not have died." (John 11:17–21)

In the ancient Jewish culture, the fourth day after a person's death carried a lot of significance. The first three days were dedicated to a practice called *Shemira*,[3] which is the ritual of watching over a deceased person's body from the time of death until burial. Those watching used the time to meditate, read Scripture, and pray.

Why three days? Because according to the Jewish tradition of that day, a deceased person's soul would hover over the body until the fourth day, when the soul would permanently separate from the body and pass into the afterlife. Only at that point was a corpse ready to be buried.

That's the situation Jesus walked into: it was the fourth day, Lazarus had been buried, and his sisters had officially lost all hope.

Can you imagine Mary and Martha's reaction as they heard the mourning crowd begin to whisper? "Jesus is here. He's come." It was Martha, likely exhausted from days of grieving, who went outside to meet Him.

I want to highlight two things about Martha in this passage. First, I genuinely love her honesty here. "Lord, if only you had been here, my brother would not have died." This wasn't the fake, Christianized language we've been taught to say in church when something bad happens—things like "He's in a better place."

No, this was real. This was genuine. Martha was hurting and angry, and she wanted Jesus to know it.

There are times we need to speak to God with that kind of honesty:

- "Lord, You could have made things better if You wanted to. Why didn't You?"
- "God, why weren't You there when I needed You? Where were You?"
- "Where were You when my loved one died?"
- "Where were You when my relationship fell apart?"

- "Where were You when I was hurt?"
- "Where were You when I prayed for that miracle?"
- "Where were You when we couldn't get pregnant?"
- "Where were You when I lost my job?"
- "Where were You when I needed You most?"
- "Where were You when my dream died?"
- *"Where were You, God?!"*

I'm proud of Martha for pouring out her heart rather than stuffing everything down and trying to be "spiritual." I hope to be that honest with God when I experience that kind of pain.

The second thing I want to point out about Martha is the presence of her expectations. Specifically, her unsurrendered expectation that Jesus *just had to* heal her brother. Can you hear it in her words? "Lord, if only you had been here." Mary and Martha had notified Jesus about Lazarus's sickness. They'd sent for Him, and they had expected Him to respond. They expected Him to come and make everything better.

But Jesus hadn't come—not soon enough, anyway. Martha's words reflect the disappointment of unsurrendered expectations. So does her grief.

Thankfully, Jesus recognized the root of her problem. He understood both her pain and her unsurrendered expectation, and He took the time to help her let go of both and trust in Him.

THE ANTIDOTE FOR DISAPPOINTMENT

To start off, Jesus told Martha what was about to happen: "Your brother will rise again" (John 11:23).

Martha was still floundering in the pain of her unsurrendered expectations—of her disappointment—and, therefore, wasn't able to hear the hope in Jesus' words. "'Yes,' Martha said, 'he will rise when everyone else rises, at the last day'" (v. 24).

But look at how Jesus responded:

> Jesus told her, "I am the resurrection and the life. Anyone who believes in me will live, even after dying. Everyone who lives in me and believes in me will never ever die. Do you believe this, Martha?" "Yes, Lord," she told him. "I have always believed you are the Messiah, the Son of God, the one who has come into the world from God." (vv. 25–27)

Do you see what Jesus did? He heard Martha's disappointment, but He didn't let her stay there. Instead, He brought her back to the key truth of her situation: that He is God. That He is in control. And that He is worthy of our trust.

That is the antidote for disappointment caused by our unsurrendered expectations: actively, deliberately choosing to trust in God even when our circumstances don't make sense—even when our circumstances still cause us pain. Remember, we wallow in disappointment when our reality continually fails to line up with our expectations. But Jesus is greater than our reality and greater than our expectations; He is the resurrection and the life.

Notice that Jesus pushed Martha to verbalize her belief. "Do you believe this, Martha?" And to Martha's credit, she responded. She acknowledged Jesus as her Lord, and she did it *before* He brought a miracle into her life—before He fulfilled her dream.

Ten years ago, one of my closest friends, a man named Roman, went through a horrible tragedy when his mother was struck by a car and killed during her morning prayer walk.

Roman went through all the emotions people go through when they lose someone they love so deeply—but he never walked away from his faith or doubted the character of God. I'm in awe of his faith, and I recently asked him how he found the strength to worship God after such a horrible loss. He told me: "If I believe God came to earth as a man named Jesus so that I could go to heaven, why would I reject Him? He's given my mom the reward of heaven."

> **JESUS IS GREATER THAN OUR REALITY AND GREATER THAN OUR EXPECTATIONS; HE IS THE RESURRECTION AND THE LIFE.**

Those of us who follow God need to remember, like Roman, that our faith in Jesus isn't based on our circumstances. Christianity isn't circumstantial. We have to be careful not to allow our limited knowledge—or our expectations of how things are *supposed* to be—to get in the way of our hope for the future.

Because when we least expect it, Jesus might show up and ask us to roll aside the stone:

> "Roll the stone aside," Jesus told them. But Martha, the dead man's sister, protested, "Lord, he has been dead for four days. The smell will be terrible." Jesus responded, "Didn't I tell you that you would see God's glory if you believe?" So they rolled the stone aside. Then Jesus looked

up to heaven and said, "Father, thank you for hearing me."
(vv. 39–41)

I think it's interesting that Jesus told Martha and Mary to participate in rolling the stone away from Lazarus's grave. He wanted them to do it with their own hands. Why? Because Jesus was inviting them to participate in their miracle. It's not as if Jesus couldn't move the stone on His own; it's that He wanted to see their obedience before they experienced the resurrection of their hope. He wanted them to overcome their unsurrendered expectations by moving forward in faith, believing that even though their dream didn't turn out how they expected, when God is in control it's never too late.

So consider this: What stone is Jesus pushing you to move today? What leap of faith is He asking you to make so that you can see something you thought was dead come back to life? What unsurrendered expectation that has held you back is God asking you to surrender? Make that phone call, pray that prayer, start that business, begin that ministry, offer forgiveness, and dream that dream again. It's time to roll some stones!

As we conclude our journey with Mary, Martha, and Lazarus, I want to make sure we don't miss what I believe to be the most powerful moment of this story. Note the words of Jesus:

Then Jesus shouted, "Lazarus, come out!" And the dead man came out, his hands and feet bound in graveclothes, his face wrapped in a headcloth. Jesus told them, "Unwrap him and let him go!" (vv. 43–44)

Can you picture Lazarus staggering out of the tomb, his hands and feet still bound in his graveclothes? I can. (And I'm pretty sure if I had been a bystander, I would have ruined the moment by screaming "Mummy!" and running away at top speed.)

In any case, Jesus told them to unwrap Lazarus and let him go. Why didn't Jesus just drop the mic when Lazarus walked out of the tomb? Why did He tell them to unwrap his friend? Because it wasn't enough for Lazarus to breathe again—Jesus wanted him to shed every appearance of death. Overcoming death was just a step in the journey to what John called "life that is truly life," and Jesus wanted Lazarus to live!

Even in the pain of disappointment, a part of you may recognize, as Martha did, that Jesus is the Messiah. He's the one whose resurrection built a bridge between our lives on earth and an eternity with God. But there's more good news: you don't have to live in hell while waiting for eternity in heaven. Jesus told His disciples that "the Kingdom of God is already among you" (Luke 17:21). He wants us to experience the benefits of salvation here and now. Hope, freedom, joy—these can be ours today as a result of walking with God, following His principles, and trusting in His plan for us.

How often we miss this truth!

After years of lost hope, broken relationships, depression, addictions, disappointment, shame, and broken dreams, we have slowly dressed ourselves in graveclothes. We're breathing, but we're wrapped in the weight of our pasts. We've allowed ourselves to be defeated in our expectations, and our hearts are sick.

When we find ourselves in that situation—disappointed

and struggling to dream—we have a choice. We can sit in discouragement and wait for heaven, or we can begin removing the graveclothes *right now* and live the life God has always intended for us.

Let me ask you in this moment: Are you a wounded eagle? Have you allowed yourself to settle for a stump because of the injuries you received from unsurrendered expectations? From disappointment?

Or are you ready to soar?

Jesus is ready to lift you up. He's ready to show you the amazing, incredible, unbelievable life He planned for you before He set the foundations of the world. You are not the sum of your mistakes, you are not used up, and you are not a failure.

It's time to spread your wings and soar in faith. It's time to surrender your expectations to God, roll away some stones, and fight against the destructive inclination to dress yourself in the graveclothes of yesterday.

WE HAVE TO BE CAREFUL

NOT TO ALLOW OUR LIMITED

KNOWLEDGE—OR OUR

EXPECTATIONS OF HOW

THINGS ARE *SUPPOSED* TO

BE—TO GET IN THE WAY OF

OUR HOPE FOR THE FUTURE.

three

SAWZALL THE WALL

The very nature of joy makes nonsense of our common distinction between having and wanting.

—C. S. LEWIS[1]

"Why do you have a hammer?" There was mild curiosity in my wife's voice—until she looked down at my other hand. Then I heard mild concern. "Is that a saw?"

"It's called a Sawzall," I said.

"Okay . . ." Jennifer responded, still concerned. "Why are you bringing those in here at 8:00 p.m. on a Sunday?"

Great question, but I had a great answer. Just an hour before, Jennifer and I had been snuggling on the couch and enjoying *Fixer Upper* together on HGTV. We'd watched in wonder as Chip and Joanna Gaines, the hosts of the show, transformed an outdated house into a modern dream home.

The biggest change happened when Chip and his crew took down several walls on the main floor to create an open living space. What had once been dark and closed off was now bright and free-flowing.

Watching that episode, I had been overcome by the awareness that my home was dark and closed off as well. The people on TV had received this amazing gift from the Gaineses, but what about my own wife and children? Was I going to allow them to continue to be trapped in little boxes when they could have a house that was open and free? No, I was not! I had made my decision, I had retrieved my hammer and Sawzall, and now I was ready to act.

Secure in my plan, I pointed at the wall separating our kitchen from the living room and told Jennifer, "We both like the idea of an open-concept living space. So I'm going to tear down that wall."

"You're going to start a construction project *now*?" she asked. Mild concern was long gone; major panic was close at hand. "You're not Chip Gaines!"

Whoa. The gauntlet had been thrown down. "I'm not Chip?" I repeated. "What does Chip know that I don't know?" In my mind, it was game on. Gagnon versus Gaines! Finished talking, I confidently drove my hammer through a section of drywall. Our home renovation project had begun!

A little over an hour later, I stepped back to admire my work. Every inch of drywall had been pulled free, revealing the wooden studs. So far so great! Feeling genuinely proud of myself, I texted a contractor friend of mine with some pictures of my success.

Just a few seconds later, I received a FaceTime request. It

was that same friend. "Show me the top of your wall, Josh!" he said, not even bothering with "Hello."

I angled the phone upward so he could see where the wall met the ceiling.

"Oh, thank goodness," he breathed. "I was worried you were taking down a load-bearing wall. I didn't want your house to collapse on you tonight when the wind blew."

I had tried to walk out of the room so Jennifer wouldn't hear, but one glance at her face told me I was too late. Her mouth was wide open in an O of shock.

"Hey, I appreciate the concern and the call," I told my friend. I think I managed to sound casual. "I guess that could have gone bad."

Jennifer didn't say anything. No mention of the fact that I might have been a few hammer swings away from crushing our family, which is just one of the reasons I love her so much. But we both knew the score—Chip: 1, Josh: 0. The renovation project continued over the next couple of weeks, but by the time I finished, it was pretty clear I would never host my own HGTV series.

Whatever, Chip!

As I think back on that memory, I can't help but wonder why I was so driven to take down that wall. What could have motivated me to do such a thing without any planning or even any real thought?

I'm afraid I know the answer: discontentment. When I saw how nice the project house turned out on TV, my own home suddenly seemed insufficient. Not good enough for me and my family.

I wish I could say that was the only time I've had a problem with discontentment. I struggle with discontentment every day. In fact, I've come to realize that feeling like I never have enough is my greatest vice. There is nothing that makes me more vulnerable to sin than discontentment.

RECOGNIZING DISCONTENTMENT

Here's something I've learned the hard way: discontentment is a major obstacle to achieving our God-sized dreams. That's because it constantly distracts us from our purpose—from what we are designed to desire, pursue, and achieve.

In short, discontentment takes our minds off our dreams and refocuses them on something far less important.

And what makes discontentment really insidious is that it can linger under the surface of our lives like a low-grade fever, going unnoticed and building strength until it's too late. Sure, we may recognize that we feel dissatisfied from time to time, but it's difficult to get down to the real root of the problem. As a result, many of our poor decisions, regrettable actions, and sins can be traced back to our self-centered feelings of discontentment.

Of course, these realities aren't new. You might hear a lot of fuss about how people today are hypermaterialistic and can never get enough—and there's certainly a lot of truth to those observations. However, discontentment has been a problem for the human heart almost as long as there have been human hearts. In fact, we can follow the root of our discontentment all the way back to the garden of Eden, when sin snaked its way into our world.

Adam and Eve were the masterpiece of God's creative work, designed in His image to enjoy a relationship with Him for eternity. They were perfect, and they enjoyed their perfection in a paradise called the garden of Eden. But then the Enemy, Satan, distracted Adam and Eve by pointing out what they didn't have: the forbidden fruit. The humans were no longer content with paradise and all the fruit they did have—they wanted the one thing that had been made off limits.

As a result of that basic, primal feeling of discontentment, sin has corrupted the world ever since.

Satan's strategy in the garden was to use Adam and Eve's desire for more as a way to minimize the blessings with which God had surrounded them. And Satan is still using that same method of attack today. He wants to lure us away from our God-sized dreams and our God-ordained purposes by tempting us to focus on what we don't have instead of being faithful with everything we've been given.

To see what I mean, let's look at three specific types of discontentment and see how they distract us from pursuing the life God desires for us.

Material and Financial Discontentment

One of the many things we have to deal with today that Adam and Eve did not is commercials. Unfortunately, we live in a world where businesses are constantly finding new and more invasive ways to push us toward buying what they're selling. Even more so, marketing and advertising professionals are very aware that it's human nature to desire the newest and best of everything.

This isn't a rant against marketing, and this isn't the part of the book where I suggest collecting rainwater and using it to bathe in order to be more "spiritual." It's been said before, but it's worth repeating: there is nothing wrong with having money or owning things you enjoy—but there is something wrong when your possessions own you.

If you live in a constant state of discontentment over the stuff you don't have, that's a good indication that material wealth *has* you. If your identity is wrapped up in driving the nicest car, living in the biggest house, and having the highest-paying job, you will always crave more—and you'll never find what you truly need. Because true contentment isn't found in possessions and things.

Again, these are truths you already know. If you've been in church for a while, you've likely heard dozens of sermons on this subject.

But remember: discontentment distracts us from our God-sized dreams. It points us toward what doesn't matter at the expense of what does. So it's fair to ask yourself: *Am I being distracted right now by money and material possessions? Do I spend more effort chasing stuff or pursuing my God-sized dreams? Does the need to maintain a certain lifestyle hinder me from accomplishing what God designed me to do for His kingdom?*

Relational Discontentment

In my years of ministry, I've encountered many people who've been derailed in the pursuit of their dreams because they live in relational discontentment. This plays out in myriad ways, but the core problem is always the same: believing that the grass is greener on the other side of the fence.

For example, sometimes single people will repeatedly give

their bodies away in the hope of finding contentment through being wanted by someone. Sometimes married people invest countless hours on social media wishing their spouses were more like _____. Or sometimes people spend a lifetime secretly watching pornography in an effort to find contentment through a counterfeit relationship.

Just as Adam and Eve were curious about the unknown taste of the forbidden fruit, we also are too often excited by the possibilities of something—or someone—new and different in our relationships. One thing I've learned through my role as a pastor is that marriage counseling is *hard*. In fact, it's often painful. I've seen firsthand what happens when couples spend more time watering the lawn of their lust than the lawn of their marriage. Misdirected attention will almost inevitably lead to separation, and it always causes significant damage.

Obviously, there are a lot of negative consequences from relational strife itself, but sometimes we forget how those consequences radiate outward. Specifically, we forget that discontentment in our relationships is just another distraction that hinders us from pursuing our God-sized dreams.

Adultery and pornography and emotional affairs and sexual immorality are all harmful enough in their own right. But they are all based in discontentment, which means they all distract us from what matters most and the dreams God has placed in our hearts.

Discontentment with Circumstances

As I mentioned earlier, much of our modern society is built on consumerism, which is the continual desire to get more stuff. Obviously, this is prime fuel for discontentment.

But this cultural obsession doesn't stop at material goods. Our culture is also built on continually upgrading our circumstances. That can include our careers, our social standing, our social media influence, our political influence, our education, our relationships, and so on. As a society, we are constantly on the lookout for ways to make ourselves seem and feel more impressive. More cultured. More successful.

Again, I need to make it clear that it's not wrong or sinful to have a good career or an excellent education or zillions of followers online. Those things in and of themselves are not the problem. Instead, the problem is when we try to use those external factors as a way to find contentment or happiness—because that won't work.

We often chase contentment by trying to change our circumstances. When we're dissatisfied with our lives, we tend to look at our surroundings and ask ourselves, *What could I change to make myself happier?* We change jobs, friends, marriages, churches, houses, vehicles, and a plethora of other things, all in an attempt to unlock joy and fulfillment and contentment.

Why is that a problem? Contentment is never found in external circumstances; it's only found internally as a result of a growing relationship with Jesus. It's internal, not external.

As the apostle Paul wrote: "I know how to live on almost nothing or with everything. I have learned the secret of living in every situation, whether it is with a full stomach or empty, with plenty or little. For I can do everything through Christ, who gives me strength" (Phil. 4:12–13).

Contentment can be found in Jesus alone; however, it's very hard for me as a Christ follower to actually live out that belief. I often search for joy, hope, satisfaction, and fulfillment in my career, relationships, and accomplishments. It's not until those avenues come up short over and over that I find myself asking my heavenly Father to help me find contentment in the right places once again: His love, His guidance, His opinion of me, and His plan for my life. One of the truths I've seen play out in my life is that every time I find myself attempting to chase contentment by changing my circumstances, I also find myself distracted from pursuing my God-sized dreams.

> CONTENTMENT IS NEVER FOUND IN EXTERNAL CIRCUMSTANCES; IT'S ONLY FOUND INTERNALLY AS A RESULT OF A GROWING RELATIONSHIP WITH JESUS.

THE SECRET POWER OF "JUST ENOUGH"

We've seen that discontentment is dangerous to our dreams because it distracts us. It removes our focus from what is most important and, instead, causes us to chase after more stuff, more fulfilling relationships, better circumstances, and so on.

So what can we do about it? How do we stop ourselves from being distracted and discontent?

To find the answer, let's take a look at the book of Proverbs, which is an ancient collection of wisdom found in the Bible. Here's what one of the authors of Proverbs had to say on the subject of contentment:

> O God, I beg two favors from you; let me have them before
> I die. First, help me never to tell a lie. Second, give me nei-
> ther poverty nor riches! Give me just enough to satisfy my
> needs. For if I grow rich, I may deny you and say, "Who is
> the LORD?" And if I am too poor, I may steal and thus insult
> God's holy name. (Prov. 30:7–9)

Not too many people in today's society would dare to ask of God what this person was begging for: "Give me just enough to satisfy my needs." That's a beautiful prayer, and it's one I wish I could pray with honesty.

The truth is, I don't want God to give me just enough to satisfy my needs; I want Him to give me what I want and a lot more! I want what others have because I think it will make me happier, more popular, and more confident in who I am. And I don't think I'm alone when it comes to living with an unquenchable thirst for having more.

Whether we admit it or not, many of us genuinely believe the grass is greener on the other side of the fence. And the more time we spend admiring everyone else's lawns, the more we neglect to nurture and maintain and appreciate our own.

Instead of constantly wishing and striving and grasping for "just a little more," we should make it our goal to rely on God for "just enough." Think of how that would change our perspectives.

With that in mind, are you ready to fight back against discontentment? For the remainder of this chapter, I want to explore several practical steps we can take to reject discontentment and the distractions it causes. In doing so, we'll find positive ways to pursue what matters most.

WATCH YOUR FOCUS

I'm going to share with you a principle that can help you resist discontentment. In fact, I believe this principle can change your perspective in a huge way.

Here it is: *what you focus on will always become magnified.*

Think of it like using a microscope or a telescope. Whatever you focus on with those instruments—whatever captures your gaze and your attention—will always become larger than life. So, if you choose to focus on others' possessions or accomplishments, they will become magnified and your life will become more insignificant in comparison. But if you choose to focus on your own talents, purpose, and future, your life will flourish and the lives of others will not be cause for discontentment.

WHAT YOU FOCUS ON WILL ALWAYS BECOME MAGNIFIED.

The New Testament tells a story about Jesus walking on water during a terrible storm while His disciples watched from (and mostly cowered in) a nearby boat. But there was one disciple who was not afraid—or at least not too afraid to realize how incredible it was that Jesus was walking on water.

Realizing the uniqueness of that moment, Peter asked Jesus if he could join Him on the water—and Jesus said yes! Peter usually gets a bad rap for what happened next, but I think it's pretty amazing that he had enough faith to get out of the boat in the first place. However, when Peter "saw the strong wind and the waves, he was terrified and began to sink" (Matt. 14:30). As Peter called out, Jesus reached out and saved him from drowning.

I want you to notice how this story unfolds. Peter walked on water when he was focused on Jesus, but he began to sink when he shifted his focus to the wind and the waves. Remember the principle from earlier? Whatever you focus on will become magnified. If you stare at the wind and the waves, they will overcome you, and you will sink. But if you turn your eyes toward Jesus, your faith will increase, and you will boldly walk forward.

This is true for every area of our lives. In order to battle discontentment and stay focused on pursuing our dreams, we have to consistently and intentionally watch where we are putting our focus. If we take our eyes off Jesus, we'll sink. Every time.

We must watch our focus as we fight to free ourselves from discontentment and pursue our dreams.

DESTROY COMPARISONS

Another way to fight back against discontentment is to destroy the tendency to compare ourselves with others—every time it rears its head.

Jennifer and I love taking the boys to the beach to search for sand dollars, ride the waves, and toss around the football. Recently, we were at one of our boys' favorite beaches, enjoying the sound of the waves, when Jennifer asked me, "Why don't you take your shirt off and get some sun?"

I looked at her and winked. "After all these years you still want to see me with my shirt off, huh?" She laughed, but I was feeling good. Feeling confident.

About two minutes later, a guy who looked strikingly like

Fabio started setting up his chair and umbrella right beside us. (If you don't know who Fabio is, google "I can't believe it's not butter." You'll know who I'm talking about.) This muscled mutant hadn't even brought a shirt to the beach—he may not have even owned one!

For the next hour, whenever I saw that guy sitting there, I was reminded of how quickly my hair is falling out and how my six-pack was stolen by Chinese food. Needless to say, I was no longer feeling good *or* confident.

That's why comparison is such a filthy trap! It robs us of our joy and breeds discontentment, which again distracts us from pursuing our God-sized dreams.

Sadly, when we don't feel confident or content in our own skin, we often try to overcome those feelings by comparing our lives with those around us. We love metrics, gauges, grades, raises, and scoreboards because they give us tools by which to measure our worth. That's another reason we gravitate toward comparison: it serves as our measuring stick.

As a life-giving and relevant book, the Bible has this to say about our tendency to compare ourselves with others: "Pay careful attention to your own work, for then you will get the satisfaction of a job well done, and you won't need to compare yourself to anyone else" (Gal. 6:4).

Do you want to have satisfaction? Would you like to be content with who you are? Then "pay careful attention to your own work." Or, in the context of this book, pay careful attention to your own dreams. Because if you diligently pursue your God-sized dreams, you'll find contentment in achieving what God has planned for you—and you'll destroy the need to compare yourself with others.

DON'T GIVE IN TO HUNGER PANGS

Do you ever get hungry when you're bored? I do. All the time, actually. I'll be working away in the office, maybe on a task I'm not too excited about—and then, all of a sudden, I'll feel this intense hunger. *I'm starving!*

The reality, of course, is that I'm not starving. I'm not even hungry—not really. What's happening is that I've trained my body to associate snacks with fun, so when I need a little more excitement in my life, it triggers a desire within my body to "snap into a Slim Jim!"

There's a similar dynamic that often comes into play when we experience discontentment. As we explored above, most of us have trained ourselves to deal with discontentment by changing something in our lives—changing our circumstances, changing our relationships, changing our stuff, and so on. Therefore, much like I experience hunger pangs when I'm bored, discontentment can produce in us a strong desire to experience something new. Something exciting or euphoric.

Here's how this looks on a practical level: If I'm feeling discontent about my financial situation, I might experience a "hunger pang" where I'm tempted to spontaneously buy something new or open a credit card. Someone who feels relational dissatisfaction might feel tempted to engage in an emotional affair, participate in sexual activity, watch pornography, or pursue countless other mistakes. Someone who feels discontentment regarding her circumstances might have a "hunger pang" that drives her to plan a hasty vacation or take an unnecessary risk just to experience something new.

As a side note, these hunger pangs are often the source of what we jokingly refer to as a midlife crisis. Lots of people feel discontent as they move into their forties and fifties. Life isn't going how they planned, they feel dissatisfied, and so they chase a quick adrenaline rush by purchasing a sports car or taking up skydiving or some other extreme thing.

Just as he did with Adam and Eve, Satan continually tries to deceive us into solving the temporary problem of feeling discontent by making a terrible decision that leads to ruin and derails us from pursuing our dreams. I don't know what forbidden fruit the Enemy is dangling in front of you right now, but I know with 100 percent certainty that you'll be much better off if you reject that hunger pang and address the deeper issues behind your discontentment.

Let's look at how the Bible approaches this topic in the book of James:

> God blesses those who patiently endure testing and temptation. Afterward they will receive the crown of life that God has promised to those who love him. And remember, when you are being tempted, do not say, "God is tempting me." God is never tempted to do wrong, and he never tempts anyone else. Temptation comes from our own desires, which entice us and drag us away. These desires give birth to sinful actions. And when sin is allowed to grow, it gives birth to death. (James 1:12–15)

If you want to find peace and purpose in your life—if you want to pursue your God-sized dreams—you must deny the hunger pangs of temptation and resist the counterfeit fruit of false contentment. Don't fuel the fire; instead, run as far away from it as possible.

For example, if you know that Facebook creates envy within you, consider deleting your account. At the very least, find concrete ways to spend less time there on a daily basis. If a coworker is giving you attention that you know may lead to bad decisions, don't passively let it happen and linger on the edge of making a mistake. Sooner or later, that edge will crumble! Be clear and vocal about your values and reject any advances. If necessary, change departments or even find a new job.

These things may seem extreme because they go against our human nature—the way we're taught to think culturally. But if you want to be content with your life, you must deny the hunger pangs that come your way, and you must do so every time they arise. Chasing your dreams may cause momentary feelings of discontentment as you are forced to give up an immediate pleasure, but you can push through to experience the joy of a dream fulfilled.

REPLACE ENTITLEMENT WITH GRATITUDE

My final strategy for fighting back against discontentment is to replace our feelings of entitlement with gratitude.

What do I mean by "entitlement"? Well, when we are feeling discontent about one or more areas of our lives, we often dwell on all the reasons we don't deserve to be in that situation—all the reasons we deserve better. We think about how unfairly we are being treated. We grumble about all the reasons things should be different and all the ways we are being misused or misunderstood.

In general, when we experience discontentment with our lives, we have a tendency to pout. And often, our pouting can lead to full-blown despair—both of which will sidetrack us from pursuing our dreams.

There's a remarkable story in the Bible about Paul and Silas being arrested for publicly praying in the name of Jesus. After being stripped of their clothes and severely beaten, Paul and Silas were thrown into the inner dungeon of the jail. Then Scripture tells us:

> Around midnight Paul and Silas were praying and singing hymns to God, and the other prisoners were listening. Suddenly, there was a massive earthquake, and the prison was shaken to its foundations. All the doors immediately flew open, and the chains of every prisoner fell off! The jailer woke up to see the prison doors wide open. He assumed the prisoners had escaped, so he drew his sword to kill himself.
>
> But Paul shouted to him, "Stop! Don't kill yourself! We are all here!" The jailer called for lights and ran to the dungeon and fell down trembling before Paul and Silas.
>
> Then he brought them out and asked, "Sirs, what must I do to be saved?"
>
> They replied, "Believe in the Lord Jesus and you will be saved, along with everyone in your household." (Acts 16:25–31)

Can you imagine that? Paul and Silas were praying and singing to God even after they'd been beaten and imprisoned for doing His work.

I'm embarrassed to say that if I had been either of them, I would have sat in that dungeon and complained. I would have listed all the reasons I shouldn't have been there. I would have said entitled things such as: "Thanks a lot, Jesus. Here I am traveling the countryside sharing Your message, and I'm getting beaten for it. I don't deserve this. I deserve better." I would have wallowed in self-pity, complaining about how far off course I was from my dreams and how undeserving I was of these horrible circumstances.

Yes, I would have pouted. And as a result, I would have remained in jail a lot longer than Paul and Silas did. I believe that the key that unlocked their prison door was gratitude. Their praise to God in spite of their circumstances set them free and positioned them perfectly to continue pursuing their God-sized dreams.

If you feel as though you're in a dungeon of discontentment, don't pout. Don't allow yourself to drift into despair. Instead, it's time to step outside the ordinary and into the extraordinary. Start praising God for everything you have instead of dwelling on what you wish was different. Start thanking Him for the fact that, even though you're not where you want to be, you're also not where you could be.

That's how you fight back against discontentment. Remember, God can handle your grief and your anger when you experience genuine crises in life, so never be afraid to pour out your heart to Him. But when it comes to avoiding discontentment, we'll have better success by choosing gratitude.

So, instead of wallowing in dissatisfaction about where you live, thank God that you have a roof over your head. Instead of complaining about your car, thank Him that you have any transportation at all. Instead of griping about your family, thank God that you have someone to love. Instead of whining about your job, thank Him that you have a way to make money. Instead of complaining about what God has not yet done, thank Him for what He has given you in Jesus. Thank Him for every blessing you can think of, and you will begin to feel contentment rise within your soul.

Pro tip: you can't be thankful and discontent at the same time. Those concepts are mutually exclusive. As you shift your perspective and begin to live in thankfulness, your level of joy will increase. Simply put, gratitude sustains our joy. When you're fighting to find joy and contentment, start thanking God for all the blessings you have. Even if you're still waiting on some miracles, thank Him for the ones you've already received.

I love this verse in Ecclesiastes 6:9: "Enjoy what you have rather than desiring what you don't have. Just dreaming about nice things is meaningless—like chasing the wind." Let your praise unlock the doors that are seemingly shut and locked!

I realize that I'll have to fight against discontentment for the rest of my life. But that's a fight I'm willing to make because my dreams are worth it. The plan and purpose God has placed in front of me are worth it.

The same is true for you. As you let go of disappointment and throw yourself into pursuing your God-sized dreams, don't allow the Enemy to distract you with discontentment. Fight back! Say no! And savor a life sustained by joy and gratitude.

WHEN YOU'RE FIGHTING
TO FIND JOY AND
CONTENTMENT, START
THANKING GOD FOR
ALL THE BLESSINGS
YOU HAVE.

four

PREDICTABLE RESISTANCE

Many of us have two lives. The life we live, and the unlived
life within us. Between those two stands resistance.

—STEVEN PRESSFIELD[1]

"Hello, everyone! I'm Josh Gagnon, and I can't even express
how excited I am to see each of you here this morning at the
launch of our new church!"

It was my first service at Next Level Church, and I was so
excited. I mean, I was pumped! I was finally witnessing the
first stages of my dream being fulfilled, and I was ready for
God to pour out His Holy Spirit and shake the walls of the
high school auditorium we'd rented for that first gathering.

Unfortunately, there didn't seem to be anyone in the congregation who shared my enthusiasm, because my greeting
got no response—no cheers, no applause, not even a polite

"Amen." If I had been a comedian, I would have said, "Wow, tough crowd," and then told my best joke about the president. (That always eases the tension in a room, right?)

Since I'm a pastor, however, I pressed on with my message. I told everyone in attendance that we were about to experience God's blessings—that our church would one day expand outward to many locations and that our ministries would affect thousands of people by connecting them with the gospel of Jesus Christ.

I looked out over the gathering as I spoke, but there was still very little response. People stared at me with rigid backs and stony faces. Every now and then someone readjusted themselves in their seat—I'm sure those high school chairs weren't super comfortable—but that was about as exciting as things got.

I remember thinking, *It's as if they're all numb to what God can do. They don't realize God can still do the impossible!*

After church, a woman I'd never met approached me, put her hand on my arm, and said, "I've lived in New England my entire life, and I've seen many pastors come and go. What you're planning to do here will never work. People don't even want the kind of church you're talking about. It's going to be sad to see all your passion go to waste."

Ouch! Those few sentences were tough enough, but I quickly learned she was just getting warmed up. For the next few minutes, she explained with point-by-point efficiency all the reasons I was bound to fail and why I should just give up. It was a discouraging conversation to say the least, and her negative words practically knocked the wind out of me.

Thankfully, I didn't give up. I'm still having a blast pursuing my dreams by serving God at NLC. But that woman's words will always stay with me as a reminder that nothing important happens in our lives without some measure of resistance.

UNDERSTANDING RESISTANCE

So far we've explored several obstacles that can derail us from pursuing our dreams if we allow them to. We began by discussing the way unsurrendered expectations can cause disappointment in our lives, which is a major factor in people surrendering their ability to dream. We've also examined how discontentment distracts us from pursuing those dreams by demanding that we give our attention to what's less important.

In this chapter, I want to help you get a better understanding of the resistance you will face when you choose to pursue your dreams. And please note that I didn't say you *might* face resistance or you *may* face it. No, I used the words *you will* intentionally, because resistance is inevitable whenever we choose to pursue anything worthwhile.

What do I mean by "resistance"? Good question. Let me try to answer it.

Imagine you're striding along one of those moving walkways installed in lots of airports today. When you are moving in the same direction as the walkway, everything is great, right? You get carried along faster and with less energy required than walking on your own.

But now imagine turning around and trying to walk the opposite way. Can you feel how hard that would be? You would have to pick up your pace just to stay in the same place. You could move forward if you wanted to, but you would have to expend a huge amount of energy to make any progress—and you'd probably have to dodge all the people whizzing by in the normal direction, which wouldn't help your progress or popularity. Pretty soon, you'd feel tempted to turn around and let the walkway carry you along its path rather than trudge forward toward your goal.

That's resistance. Or at least, that's what it feels like in the context of pursuing our God-sized dreams and desired futures. Resistance is a force that constantly tries to push us back whenever we start making progress toward our goals. And the faster we try to move forward and the more we achieve, the greater resistance we feel.

(By the way, don't actually try to go the opposite direction on a moving walkway. Just trust me on that. I speak from experience.)

There are a couple of ways we typically experience resistance as we pursue our dreams, and one of them is through other people. Let me warn you now: when you start sharing your God-sized dream with others, be prepared for people to try to talk you out of what you see for your future—and be prepared for them to try to talk you into living a safe, ordinary life that's far away from dreams that are way too big for them to understand. Sometimes people do this through a well-meaning desire to be helpful; other times their motives are more mean-spirited. But just know that it *will* happen.

I remember the first time it happened to me. I was twenty-six years old and standing on the tenth tee box at the Nippo Lake Golf Club with my pastor at the time, a man I loved and whose opinion I deeply valued. I had been waiting for months to tell him about my dream of launching a church, but—although he was my spiritual role model and I knew him well—I was nervous to share this dream with him because I feared feeling rejected if he didn't agree with my vision for the future.

After sweating through the first nine holes and building up my courage, I knew it was now or never. "Pastor," I said, "I need to tell you something."

"Yeah, what's up?" he replied, pulling a fairway wood from his bag.

"I feel like God has called me to be a pastor." *Whew! I'd done it!* I told him all about my God-sized dream and all the fears and insecurities that came with it.

Then I waited for him to respond.

He was quiet for a long time, focused on his shot. Then he swung, hooking the ball to the left and landing it in the woods out of play. His face was grim when he turned to me and said eleven words I will never forget: "No, Josh, I don't think you're called into full-time ministry."

Oh no, I thought. *It's happening!* The first person who'd heard about my God-given, God-sized dream had shot it down like a clay pigeon.

To this day, I still wonder whether my pastor would've had a different response had he hit a better ball off the fairway. I guess I'll never know. But I do remember finishing the last eight holes holding back tears and fighting against the voices whispering lies in my head, trying to convince me that I had no reason to dream, no reason to believe God could do a miracle in my ordinary life.

Today, I don't harbor any bitterness toward that pastor; I

believe his criticism was well-meaning. In the end, though, he was wrong, and his words—just like those from the lady on our launch day at NLC—were just another form of resistance I needed to push through in order to pursue and accomplish my dreams.

The second type of resistance we often experience is from circumstances—from the ups and downs of life. These circumstances can be financial, political, social, personal, and so on. They can be minor or major. But they often pop up at just the right time to make us question our ability to achieve our dreams, or whether we even have the right dreams in mind in the first place.

For example, about a year after launching Next Level Church, I found myself on my bathroom floor, crying my eyes out because I felt like such a failure. Jennifer and I believed God was behind our desire to start the church, but there were major financial hurdles that were getting harder and harder to overcome. We'd already sold our house and one of our cars. I sold jewelry at pawn shops in order to pay rent. Then I had to borrow money for groceries so my family could eat.

That morning on the bathroom floor, I remember screaming at the top of my lungs, "God, please take away this dream! Please let me do something else so I can provide for my family!"

But God knew what He was doing. He knew the plan, and He kept that dream in my heart. After about an hour on the bathroom floor, I came out with enough strength to face the next day. I wish I could say that was the only time I've asked God to change my dreams or let me give up, but it's not. Each time it's happened, though, God has given me the strength to keep going.

Today, Next Level Church has nine different campuses, and I continue to learn that God's strength is always enough—no matter what circumstances we face.

RESISTANCE IS NORMAL

For the remainder of this chapter, I'd like to walk you through some principles that will help you recognize and handle resistance as you pursue your God-sized dreams. And the very first principle you need to know is that resistance is normal.

When we experience resistance for the first time—or even for the fifth or fiftieth time—it's easy for us to interpret it as a sign that something has gone wrong or that something out of the ordinary is happening. Here's how it often works: we start to travel down the road toward a God-sized dream, we meet resistance that tries to push us off track, and we think, *Oh no! I must be doing something wrong.* Not true.

In reality, experiencing resistance is often proof that you are heading in the right direction. That's because resistance isn't random. Evil really exists in the world, and you really do have an Enemy, Satan, who is vehemently opposed to God's plan and purposes in your life. The Bible says Satan "prowls around like a roaring lion, looking for someone to devour" (1 Peter 5:8). Often, the best way for Satan to "devour" you is to knock you off course from pursuing and achieving your God-inspired dreams.

> EXPERIENCING RESISTANCE IS OFTEN PROOF THAT YOU ARE HEADING IN THE RIGHT DIRECTION.

David is a great example of someone who experienced resistance *because* he was moving in the right direction. You remember the story of David and Goliath, right? The young boy who killed a giant with just a sling and a stone? Well, there are some interesting details in the context of that story that are worth calling out.

For one thing, it's important to remember that David had already been anointed as the next king of Israel *before* he went out to fight Goliath. (See 1 Samuel 16:1–13.) Because the current king, Saul, had disqualified himself in several ways, God instructed Samuel to find and anoint a replacement king from outside of Saul's family. David was that replacement.

In effect, it was David's God-sized dream to one day become king.

Why is that important? Because it helps us understand why David wanted to confront Goliath in the first place. David wasn't just a little punk looking for a fight. No, he understood himself to be the future king of God's people. Therefore, when an enemy decided to attack God's people and even slander the name of God Himself, David took action. He knew he was responsible for defending both his kingdom and the name of his God.

Yet look what happened when David showed up to the scene of the battle:

> But when David's oldest brother, Eliab, heard David talking to the men, he was angry. "What are you doing around here anyway?" he demanded. "What about those few sheep you're supposed to be taking care of? I know about your pride and deceit. You just want to see the battle!" (1 Sam. 17:28)

See that? As soon as David started to take interest in Goliath and what was going on, David's own brother tried to shoo him away. That's resistance. (Also, David's brother was probably still upset that he had been passed over as the next king. Get over it, Eliab!)

David also experienced resistance from Saul, the current king:

"Don't worry about this Philistine," David told Saul. "I'll go fight him!"

"Don't be ridiculous!" Saul replied. "There's no way you can fight this Philistine and possibly win! You're only a boy, and he's been a man of war since his youth." (vv. 32–33)

Remember, Saul was the king at the time, which means he should have been the one to face Goliath—he had been chosen by God to lead His people. Instead, Saul cowered behind his armies and did nothing. Worse, when David announced his intention to slay the giant, Saul became an agent of resistance by trying to tell David all the reasons why his dream was impossible.

There's one more element to David's story that we sometimes miss:

Then Saul gave David his own armor—a bronze helmet and a coat of mail. David put it on, strapped the sword over it, and took a step or two to see what it was like, for he had never worn such things before.

"I can't go in these," he protested to Saul. "I'm not used to them." So David took them off again. (vv. 38–39)

David wasn't interested in pursuing his dream in Saul's armor; he wanted to walk forward in his own God-given image. When you pursue a God-sized dream, people will often give you advice or encourage you to move forward in the way that seems best to them—how they would do it. But God isn't calling you forward as a pretend version of yourself, and He's not interested in your living the way others want to see you live. God is asking you to chase your dreams, slay your giants, and fight through resistance exactly as the person He uniquely created you to be.

> GOD IS ASKING YOU TO CHASE YOUR DREAMS, SLAY YOUR GIANTS, AND FIGHT THROUGH RESISTANCE EXACTLY AS THE PERSON HE UNIQUELY CREATED YOU TO BE.

In the end, David pushed through the resistance and conquered the giant—all because he had faith in God and the dream God had placed in his heart. That faith allowed him to stand within his God-given image and keep moving forward.

You'll need to do the same thing if you want to pursue your God-sized dreams. Because resistance *will* come. It's normal. It's to be expected when you begin heading in the right direction.

RESISTANCE IS OFTEN REQUIRED

Actually, not only is resistance normal, but it's often a *required* part of pursuing our dreams. Pushing through the resistance we face often strengthens us and changes us in ways that are necessary for achieving our dreams.

Think about how airplanes fly. When you're sitting on a plane and the pilot says, "Flight attendants, prepare for departure," what happens next? The pilot engages the engines, which creates thrust. That thrust pushes the plane forward along the runway—but it's not pushing through nothing. The plane is pushing through air, which means there's resistance involved. Then, at a certain point, the plane goes fast enough for the wings to change the direction and pressure of that air, of that resistance, and convert it to lift, which makes the plane go up.[2] And then, about thirty minutes later, you get to enjoy a few gulps of soda and a tiny bag of pretzels.

Planes cannot fly without pushing through the resistance generated when they move through air. In the same way, it's often impossible for us to achieve our God-sized dreams until we encounter and overcome a certain level of resistance.

How does that work on a practical level? Let me show you through the story of another young man in the Bible: Joseph.

In Genesis 37, we get a picture of Joseph's God-sized dream—and in this case, it was literally a dream:

> One night Joseph had a dream, and when he told his brothers about it, they hated him more than ever. "Listen to this dream," he said. "We were out in the field, tying up bundles of grain. Suddenly my bundle stood up, and your bundles all gathered around and bowed low before mine!"
>
> His brothers responded, "So you think you will be our king, do you? Do you actually think you will reign over us?" And they hated him all the more because of his dreams and the way he talked about them.
>
> Soon Joseph had another dream, and again he told his

brothers about it. "Listen, I have had another dream," he said. "The sun, moon, and eleven stars bowed low before me!" (vv. 5–9)

Like David, Joseph received a call from God to do something big. God made it clear that He was preparing Joseph to wield a high level of authority later in his life.

Now, you can make a pretty good case that Joseph didn't handle things well when it came to sharing his dream with others. He was actually a bit of a brat about it—but that's the point I want to make. At the moment Joseph received his God-sized dream, he wasn't ready to achieve it. He needed to grow and mature before he could handle the responsibility God planned to give him, and resistance was the method God used to spark that growth and maturity.

Specifically, Joseph encountered resistance when his brothers tried to kill him.

When they were out in an isolated field together, after an extended argument about what to do with him, Joseph's brothers beat him up and threw him down into a dry well. (See Genesis 37:18–24.) Some of the brothers wanted to kill Joseph right then and there. But one brother, Judah, was a little more practical. "'What will we gain by killing our brother? We'd have to cover up the crime. Instead of hurting him, let's sell him to those Ishmaelite traders. After all, he is our brother—our own flesh and blood!' And his brothers agreed" (vv. 24–27).

(As a side note, I bet it was pretty stressful for Joseph, huddled alone down in that well, to hear that conversation. I can imagine him hearing Judah's speech and then crying out,

"I agree! Hey! Can you hear me? I'm good with any plan that involves not killing me!")

Do you see the resistance Joseph faced? He'd been given this dream by God, and then almost immediately he was beaten, threatened *by his own family*, and then sold as a slave to Egypt. The resistance didn't stop there either. Joseph was made the servant of an Egyptian named Potiphar, and the young Israelite did well. Joseph did so well, in fact, that he was put in charge of Potiphar's entire household. But just when life started to feel positive again, Potiphar's wife tried to seduce Joseph into an affair—and when he refused, she accused him of rape and had him thrown in jail.

That's a key theme of Joseph's life. Each time he got close to achieving a dream, resistance rose up and knocked him back down again.

Do you ever feel like that? Does it sometimes seem as though you are pushed two steps back for every positive step toward your dreams? If so, don't allow yourself to despair or give up. God is fully capable of using those steps backward— using that resistance—to strengthen you and create lift in your life.

That's exactly what He did for Joseph.

While he was in prison, Joseph met a man who served Pharaoh, the king of Egypt. And through a long string of circumstances—none of which were coincidences—Joseph was able to warn Pharaoh about a famine that was going to engulf the land of Egypt and all the surrounding countries for seven years. As a result, Joseph was placed in charge of preparing the entire country for that famine. Basically, he became second in command over the entire kingdom, which meant he achieved the authority and influence God had promised him all the way back in those dreams he had experienced as a boy.

There's more to the story as well. Joseph was able to rescue the land of Egypt and other surrounding countries from what would have been a deadly famine. And can you guess who traveled to Egypt to buy food when the famine was at its worst? That's right—Joseph's brothers. Eventually, his father came as well. They were all rescued by Joseph's wise planning, and they all bowed to him in respect.

Thus, Joseph's dream came true! But that dream was many years in the making, and it required Joseph to push his way through a ton of resistance before he was ready to achieve it.

There's a powerful moment toward the end of Joseph's story when he met with his brothers shortly after their father's death. Understandably, his brothers feared that Joseph carried a grudge against them; they even thought he might use his power to kill them now that their father was dead. But here's how Joseph summarized his entire life story of pushing through resistance—including the evil actions of his brothers—to achieve his God-given dream: "You intended to harm me, but God intended it all for good. He brought me to this position so I could save the lives of many people" (Gen. 50:20).

Though Joseph faced great resistance, God used that resistance to position Joseph for His purpose. It's as if Joseph was saying, "You may have thought you were in control, but God was in control. God gave me the dream, God allowed me to face resistance, and God prepared me for His purpose."

Here's another truth about chasing God-sized dreams: we'll rarely have the opportunity to fly without meeting resistance. For most of us, the only way to achieve our dreams is through struggle. Through pushing forward even when it's tough. Remember: it's not the absence of resistance that results in dreams coming true; instead, it's developing a deep resilience that never bows in the face of adversity.

Resistance can propel us to our greatest success when we harness it instead of fearing it. God-sized dreams, God-sized comebacks, and God-sized miracles almost always require a trip down the road of resistance. Eventually, this path can take us places we'd never reach without the hardships that strengthen us and help propel us forward.

So don't be concerned when you face resistance; be determined. In fact, you should probably be concerned if you face no resistance whatsoever as you pursue your dreams. A lack of resistance usually means no new ground is being taken.

THE DIFFERENCE BETWEEN RESISTANCE AND REDIRECTION

I don't want to end this chapter without making it clear that not all negative feedback is a form of resistance. Sometimes we really are pursuing the wrong dream, and sometimes people care about us enough to tell us the truth even when it hurts, which can help us redirect our efforts toward a better goal.

So how do you tell the difference between resistance and redirection? That's a good question without an easy answer, but it basically comes down to relational equity. Meaning, has the person in question earned the right to challenge your dreams?

In my life, I never allow someone to speak into my dreams who hasn't first offered to sweat with me while I'm chasing them. In other words, not all opinions are created equal. If someone has taken the time and effort to fight, cry, and pray with me in the pursuit of a dream, that person has earned my trust, and I am much more likely to value his or her opinions.

We all need people to help and support us as we pursue our dreams. That's because there's very little of importance in this life that we can accomplish on our own. We all need a small circle of people who can speak into our dreams and help us make big decisions. Personally, I always speak with at least three of the people in my inner circle before I make any decision that is potentially life-changing.

And, as I mentioned, sometimes we need people to help us give up when we are chasing the wrong dream. There will be times when you'll need a trainer in your corner who's willing to throw in the towel when you're getting battered and bruised because you can't see beyond your own hopes, desires, and expectations.

So yes, negative feedback can be helpful. It can cause us to redirect our pursuit to something more worthwhile, which is a great thing.

Resistance, on the other hand, usually comes from people who aren't invested in your dream but who still want to share their opinions about your dream. And I've come to learn that we should run away from such opinions.

I hope you'll learn that lesson, too, and much more quickly than I did.

Oftentimes, increased resistance makes the journey that much more meaningful. I live in New Hampshire, which is a short distance to the Atlantic Ocean and about an hour from the White Mountains. There are days when Jennifer, my boys, and I hike a mountain in the morning and drive to the ocean for a swim in the afternoon. Mount Washington dominates the White Mountain landscape, dwarfing the other peaks with the highest altitude on the East Coast. It stands like a king in the heart of the Presidential Range.

There are three ways to reach the 6,289-foot summit of Mount Washington: by steam locomotive, by car, and by foot. I was a teenager the first time I took the auto road to the top, and I'll always remember the incredible views and the force of the wind. I still enjoy driving to the summit and watching as tenacious hikers crest the peak, smiling and raising their hands in triumph. I love the long-standing tradition in which people cheer for the hikers as they crest the summit.

I hiked Mount Washington for the first time in 2015, and let's just say it's more difficult than driving. It was exhausting! Hiking the trail created a lot more resistance than going by car, and I kept asking myself why I was literally *walking up a mountain* when I could enjoy a leisurely drive to the top.

But as I approached the summit, my attitude changed with the altitude. When I stared at the magnificent views, the pain in my legs felt noble. The cool air on my face felt like a well-earned prize, and I welcomed it gladly. When I finally made it to the top and heard all those lazy car-driving, train-riding people cheering at my arrival, I asked myself why anyone would ever drive a car or take a train up a mountain.

In other words, increasing the amount of resistance I experienced while working toward a goal made the achievement of that goal much sweeter and more memorable. The same can be true as we chase our God-sized dreams—when we recognize resistance for what it is and use it as motivation rather than a source of fear, we can sweeten both the pursuit of our goals and the achievement of them.

I don't know how your experiences line up with mine, but maybe even today you've faced resistance, either from people or from circumstances. Maybe you're feeling discouraged and you'd like to give up chasing after your dreams. Maybe you know exactly what I mean when I talk about going the wrong direction on a moving walkway because that's what life feels like at this very moment.

If any of those are true, don't give up! Resistance is normal. It has always stood between the now and the future when it comes to chasing after your God-sized dream. But it's temporary. And it can make you stronger if you choose to keep going.

What is that dream in your heart right now that is generating resistance? What dreams or hopes for tomorrow have you given up because the pain of resistance is too strong? Like David and Joseph, it's time for you to choose to remain faithful even in the face of that pressure. It's time for you to choose to continue pushing forward.

Because when you do, the very resistance that threatened to kill your dream and derail your future will instead become a source of strength that advances you toward a greater tomorrow.

IT'S NOT THE ABSENCE OF
RESISTANCE THAT RESULTS
IN DREAMS COMING TRUE;
INSTEAD, IT'S DEVELOPING
A DEEP RESILIENCE THAT
NEVER BOWS IN THE
FACE OF ADVERSITY.

five

WHEN LIFE HANDS YOU 4,124 LEGOS

> When we do the best that we can, we never know what
> miracle is wrought in our life, or in the life of another.
>
> —HELEN KELLER[1]

"Hey, Dad, we have something to ask you!"

Uh-oh. I was in the LEGO store with my sons, Malachi and Nehemiah, and I immediately knew what was coming: they wanted to make a deal. I could almost predict their pitch: "Dad, we'll pay back our allowance for as many weeks as it takes if you buy us this set!"

Sure enough, after we bartered over the terms for a few minutes, they brought me over to a *huge* roller-coaster set on display at the front of the store. The thing was massive! It was also extremely complicated. I saw a little sign in front of the display that read, "For expert-level builders." Then I saw a note on the box announcing that the set contained 4,124 pieces.

Honestly, my first reaction was pride that my sons wanted to tackle such an imposing set. I was impressed! But then my realistic side kicked in.

"Guys, this is way too advanced," I said. "There's no way you could finish this thing." I wasn't trying to shoot down their dreams or be mean or avoid spending money or any of that. I was giving my honest opinion. After all, from my perspective, it hadn't been that long since I was tying their shoes and wiping applesauce goo off their chins.

But my sons were having none of it. Determined to prove their ability, they walked me through section after section of the store, showing me each of the high-difficulty sets they'd already completed. "Look, Dad, this one has more than two thousand pieces, and we finished it in less than three days." "Here, Dad, we built this set two years ago, and it has almost three thousand pieces."

They were pretty convincing! And so I found myself standing in line a few minutes later with a 4,124-piece roller coaster in my hands and two smiling boys by my side. By the time we left the store, I was so proud I felt like yelling, "My sons are LEGO experts!" at the top of my lungs.

I've learned that there are two parts to a LEGO experience. The first is the "outside of the box" experience, which is where you see the fully assembled product meticulously engineered with every piece exactly where it's supposed to be. Looking at the outside of that roller-coaster box, for example, the whole thing seemed so . . . *done*. I felt confidence and pride, thinking, *Look at what my boys are going to build!*

But it's a completely different experience when you get home and open the box, because nothing inside the box is done.

The "inside of the box" experience is chaos. It's 4,124 pieces scattered across the floor—just waiting for an unwitting parent to step on them in the middle of the night—with each piece representing a moment of frustration, patience, endurance, and the ever-present possibility of failure. Watching my sons make a plan to attack that huge pile of plastic, I no longer felt confident—I felt overwhelmed, and I wasn't even part of the assembly team!

There's a similar dynamic at play when it comes to our God-sized dreams. When God first plants a dream in our hearts, it's an "outside of the box" experience. We see the vision of what He wants to accomplish in our lives—the marriage, the miracle we are praying for, the new career, peace in a certain area, victory over an addiction, and so on. In other words, we see the incredible potential of our future dreams coming true, but we see it all in its finished form. It's as if all we need to do is pick up the dream and take it to the check-out counter. *Yes, please, I'll take this one.*

When you actually start to pursue a God-sized dream, however, it becomes an "inside of the box" experience. Our dreams never arrive fully formed. They have to be chased. They have to be earned. They have to be fought for. It's as though God dumps those 4,124 pieces on the ground and says, "If you follow my directions step-by-step, trust that I'm in control, believe that I'm faithful, and persevere when things get difficult, *then* you will see this dream come true."

That's when many people say, "Wait just a minute—I hope heaven has a return policy, because I didn't sign up for this. I need fewer pieces. I want a smaller dream!"

When you find yourself at that place, as so many people do, don't give up. Don't return that desire for a greater tomorrow.

As Jesus said, count the cost. Because pursuing a God-sized dream will require a lot from you. It will take patience. It will take faith. It will take a lot of hard work. And it will require perseverance on your part to continue assembling piece after piece, walking step-by-step with God until the dream is complete.

My primary goal in writing this book is to help you move past the obstacles that have interfered with your dreams so that you can once again feel the joy of pursuing your God-inspired purpose—your God-sized dream. What we've explored together so far has really focused on the first half of that equation: moving past obstacles.

After defining God-sized dreams, we addressed how disappointment tempts us to surrender those dreams and can even shut down our ability to dream at all. Next, we saw how discouragement distracts us from pursuing our dreams, and finally, we talked about the resistance we'll face whenever we choose to chase a God-sized dream.

This chapter is a turning point, because now it's time to move into the second half of the equation I described above: learning to dream again.

TAKE THE FIRST STEP

There's a story in the Old Testament about a woman who learns how to dream again. You can find it in 2 Kings 4, and as you might imagine, the beginning of that story is pretty depressing:

> One day the widow of a member of the group of prophets came to Elisha and cried out, "My husband who served

you is dead, and you know how he feared the LORD. But now a creditor has come, threatening to take my two sons as slaves."

"What can I do to help you?" Elisha asked. "Tell me, what do you have in the house?"

"Nothing at all, except a flask of olive oil," she replied. (vv. 1–2)

We can learn a lot about this woman from these two verses. For starters, she knew what it meant to follow God, but she was frustrated and confused. Look at the first words out of her mouth: "My husband who served you is dead." Ouch! Her family had invested themselves in serving God and helping the prophets spread His message to those who needed to hear it—but things had turned sour. The woman's husband had died, had apparently left her very few possessions, and now she was in danger of losing her sons as well.

That points to the second thing we can learn about this woman: she still had a dream. Specifically, she dreamed of her family staying together and finding a place of light and peace again, rather than darkness and despair. Like so many people today, she dreamed of something hopeful for her future, but she was struggling to hold on to that dream. And in desperation, she turned to Elisha for help.

One brisk September night, I woke up around two in the morning to the sound of something scratching the walls outside my bedroom door. I sat up quickly and saw the shadow of what appeared to be a man stalking around in our hallway.

In that moment of half-awake desperation, I did the most courageous thing I could think of: I woke up my wife and whispered, "I think someone is in our house!" I was hoping that Jennifer had a secret identity as a ninja or an assassin of some kind and had been eagerly waiting years for this opportunity to show me all her skills—but no. She just stared back at me with a look that said, *What are you going to do about this?*

It was up to me. This was my moment to shine!

As I cautiously approached the bedroom door, shaking more and more with each step, I peeked into the hall through a half-closed eye. The shadow was still moving inside our hallway, silent as a ghost. Trying to make no noise, I stepped through the doorway and saw it right in front of me—a large, scary helium balloon. It was left over from my son Nehemiah's birthday party, and it was stuck in our hallway fan.

Now, I'm not typically scared of "Happy Birthday" balloons, so let me try to regain some self-respect. What happened is that my perception of the balloon as an intruder caused me to live in a false reality. It caused me to fear something that wasn't real—that wasn't true. And what we perceive, whether it's true or not, creates a reality in which we live.

In a similar way, the widow in 2 Kings 4 was living in a false reality. She had experienced a tragedy—the death of her husband and the threatened loss of her sons—and it had caused her to shut down. To live in fear and despair and hopelessness. Certainly, we can understand why she felt that way. Losing people we love will always hurt. But the danger for her, and for us, is choosing to dwell in that place of darkness for so long that it distorts our reality.

Notice what she said when Elisha asked her what she had in the house: "Nothing at all, except a flask of olive oil." That's what it feels like when we've surrendered the ability to dream—like we have nothing left. No more value. No hope for tomorrow. Just this stupid jar of olive oil.

This widow teaches us that in order to start chasing our dreams and seek out hope for tomorrow, we have to leave the false reality that has kept us grounded for so long. We have to move away from the false belief that we have nothing of value, that God doesn't answer our prayers, and that we have no reason to believe in a greater tomorrow or in a future where our dreams come true.

The truth of the situation is that this widow had Almighty God in her corner. The same God who created the universe and set the earth on its foundations. The same God who brought the Israelites out of Egypt and through the Red Sea. The same God who led His people in conquering the promised land.

The same God who stands in your corner as well, ready to support you even as you stare at all the pieces of your dream and begin to walk forward in faith toward assembling it.

If you're ready to take that first step, choose to reject once and for all the false reality that says you won't achieve your dream—that you can't achieve it. That things are hopeless. Let it go and start chasing what God has planted in your heart.

BORROW. GO. SHUT. POUR. SET.

Remember what I said before about this being the story of a woman who learned to dream again? That's why this is one of my favorite Bible moments—because she *did* choose to move forward. And the results were astounding!

Here's what happened next:

And Elisha said, "Borrow as many empty jars as you can from your friends and neighbors. Then go into your house with your sons and shut the door behind you. Pour olive oil from your flask into the jars, setting each one aside when it is filled."

So she did as she was told. Her sons kept bringing jars to her, and she filled one after another. Soon every container was full to the brim!

"Bring me another jar," she said to one of her sons.

"There aren't any more!" he told her. And then the olive oil stopped flowing.

When she told the man of God what had happened, he said to her, "Now sell the olive oil and pay your debts, and you and your sons can live on what is left over." (2 Kings 4:3–7)

This is the part of the story where God, through the prophet Elisha, handed this woman an open LEGO box and asked her to get to work. Specifically, Elisha gave her five instructions: borrow jars, go inside, shut the door, pour the oil, and set each full jar aside. Borrow, go, shut, pour, set—and then repeat.

This was a critical moment in this woman's life. Why? Because she had a choice to make. *Do I work toward seeing my dream become a reality, or do I bow down to the lies that keep telling me I have no reason to hope?*

Think about it. This woman was already exhausted. She was already grieving. She was already feeling overwhelmed and terrified at the thought of losing her sons. And then Elisha came along and asked her to go through all these extra steps. It must have been embarrassing for her to approach neighbor after neighbor and say, "Could I please borrow all of your jars?" I'm sure people asked what she wanted to use them for, and what could she say?

If I were in that woman's shoes, I would have been tempted to respond, "C'mon, Elisha. Can't you just snap your fingers and make a pile of money appear? Isn't God powerful enough to make that happen? Why do I have to jump through all these hoops?"

In truth, that's what most of us do today. We pray for instant miracles and prepackaged dreams, and then we feel discouraged when they don't appear. We live in a society that deceives us into thinking our dreams are like ninety-second rice—just put in a little bit of work, a dash of faith, a pinch of prayers, and *ta-da!* It's ready.

In fact, I was recently traveling through the town of Akureyri in Northern Iceland, and I came across this drink that was called "Little Miracles." How often we wish our hopes, dreams, and prayers could be packaged up into a single gulp!

And I say "we" intentionally, because I really don't enjoy waiting for God to move. I want my problems solved today. I don't want to wait.

But God does. God waits for us to listen. He waits for us to obey. And He waits for us to trust Him with even the tiniest amount of faith—even the size of a mustard seed, according to Jesus (Matt. 17:20). And when He sees us finally in a place where we are ready to chase that dream He's always planned for us to achieve, He gives us our box of LEGOs and our instruction book, and then He encourages us to move.

Notice how Elisha helped shift the woman's focus from what she *didn't* have to what she *did* have. Before, she looked into her house and saw "nothing at all." But Elisha helped her see what could be accomplished when she allowed God to use even the little she had for His purpose and His glory. The same is true for us! When our little is aligned with God's ultimate, it's a great recipe to witness the impossible.

Also notice how Elisha helped the woman take small steps of faith, rather than asking her to make a huge leap all at once. *Borrow. Go. Shut. Pour. Set.*

> WHEN OUR LITTLE IS ALIGNED WITH GOD'S ULTIMATE, IT'S A GREAT RECIPE TO WITNESS THE IMPOSSIBLE.

What would "borrow, go, shut, pour, set" look like in your life right now? You already know the "outside of the box" version of your dream—the final product you're chasing. But what are the practical steps God has written down in your instruction manual? What are the pieces you need to stack together with patience, obedience, and trust in His plan?

That's a key takeaway as you learn to dream again: look for those small steps God is leading you to take. Don't worry about the completion of your dream. Not yet. Not here at the beginning of your journey. Instead, concentrate on the next step in your instruction manual. Concentrate on identifying the next right thing you can do in pursuit of that dream, and then do it.

It's kind of like those Escape Room experiences that have popped up everywhere. When you are in one of those games, you wish *so badly* that you could just take one step to get out and be victorious. But no. When you find a clue, that just means you need to start looking for the next clue—and the next, and the next, and so on.

Similarly, it would be nice if God laid out His entire plan for us to pursue and achieve our dreams. Instead, God usually shows us only the next step we need to take. And we need to be willing to take that step before we'll catch a glimpse of the *next* next step. The only way to advance is to focus on the next thing in front of you and do it well.

Unfortunately, far too many people miss out on their hopes and dreams because they aren't willing to take the incremental steps required to reach them. They want to skip. They don't want to pass *Go!* but still want to collect their two hundred dollars. They want to have a cheat code that moves them to the final round without even working up a sweat. But that's not the way God operates. Look at the widow. Before she could pour the oil, she needed to borrow jars. She had to move one step at a time, and so do we.

With all that in mind, it's important to understand that there are two specific ways God works as He pours out His blessings into our lives: God-alone blessings and God-alongside blessings. Let's take a minute to explore both.

God-Alone Blessings

One of the most memorable moments of my ministry occurred during my first month of being a pastor. A woman named Nancy came by my office to tell me some heartbreaking news. She said, "Pastor Josh, I had some tests done, and the results show that I have cancer in many different places."

I could see that she was trying to keep from crying, but the dam was breaking. Tears had already started a little stream running down her cheeks.

"Let's pray and believe God can heal you of this cancer,"

I said. And as she closed her eyes and nodded in agreement, I prayed for God to heal her and to destroy every cell of that cancer in the name of Jesus Christ.

A week later, Nancy came running into my office, and I could tell right away that her burden had been lifted. I remember thinking, *Did God really?* I didn't have much time to think, though, because she screamed out, "The doctor did follow-up tests, and they can't find any cancer! It's gone! Jesus healed me!"

I'd be lying if I said I wasn't in shock. I remember asking whether her doctors were absolutely certain that she had been healed. She exclaimed, "Yes, and they are calling it a miracle!"

That's precisely what it was: a miracle. And it was a great example of what I call a God-alone blessing. God heard our prayers, and He responded in power. He stepped into an impossible situation and did what only He can do.

I actually find that it's not uncommon for God to surprise His people with those kinds of blessings. We open the mailbox and find an unexpected check; a relationship is restored; we inexplicably avoid an accident; we wake up one morning with the strength to walk away from an addiction. Or, like Nancy, we receive a miraculous physical healing.

God-alone blessings occur when we come to Him in faith—with even just a tiny mustard seed's worth of faith—and He divinely changes everything in an instant.

God-Alongside Blessings

As much as I love God-alone blessings, I've learned He also loves to provide for us in a different way—one that is equally important and far more common. I like to call this way God-alongside blessings.

These are moments of provision that occur when God invites us to participate in the outcome and join in on the excitement. We don't sit in the stands and watch things happen; rather, we're on the field playing an important role in our own stories. Could God provide the blessing without us? Of course! But I've come to realize that God doesn't pour blessings into our lives solely because of the outcome. He often wants to grow and stretch us through the journey that eventually leads to that outcome.

So, while we really appreciate the blessing that comes at the end of the journey, I believe an equal part of that blessing includes what we learn along the way and how we are transformed—how we grow and mature in the process. Our faith becomes stronger because we were a part of the blessing. We took a step of faith and saw God move mountains.

As an example, I remember the first time Malachi and Nehemiah swam from one end of an Olympic-sized pool to the other. They dove into the water and swam for their lives—quite literally in a lot of ways—and it wasn't pretty. Their arms were flailing. They made strange noises as they tried to pull their heads out of the water and gasp for air. And they probably swallowed more pool water than I or anyone cares to know.

But in the end, when they reached the other side, they beamed over at their mom with the biggest smiles on their faces. It was as if they'd just won an Olympic gold medal! It was a big moment for our family.

What our boys probably don't remember, however, is that I was in the pool as they swam. And I swam in the middle between them. When Malachi seemed to have lost his momentum and was in danger of sinking, I gave him a gentle push forward. When Nehemiah got turned around and started swimming toward the side, I guided him back. And when either of them looked as though they were getting too tired, I held them up for a moment so they could catch their breath.

In other words, reaching the other side was their achievement—their small version of a dream or a blessing—but I came alongside and helped. I supported them and made sure they achieved their goal.

That's a picture of a God-alongside blessing. And that's the way God will often help and support us as we pursue our God-sized dreams. As we move step-by-step in faithfulness, God stays with us and continues to guide us toward the goal.

LET GOD DO THE HEAVY LIFTING

There's one more detail in the widow's story that I believe is critical, and yet it's often missed. We'll find it by looking again at verse 6:

> Soon every container was full to the brim!
> "Bring me another jar," she said to one of her sons.
> "There aren't any more!" he told her. And then the olive oil stopped flowing.

The story could have easily ended after the boy said, "There aren't any more!" But no, God added that one extra detail: "And then the olive oil stopped flowing."

Bam! Do you see the power there? The widow and her sons ran out of jars before God ran out of oil! His provision never ran dry! As long as they brought jars, God filled them with grace and goodness.

What this means is that I need to let God do the heavy lifting when it comes to my dreams, especially my God-sized dreams. Yes, I need to chase those dreams. Yes, I need to take the next step and follow the previous instruction—my own version of "borrow, go, shut, pour, set." But even as I pursue my dreams in that way, I need to always remember that God is unlimited in His ability to fulfill those dreams. God is unlimited in His ability to bless me.

I never want to miss out on what God has for me. I don't want my faith to be smaller than His supply. And I certainly don't want to be the reason the oil stops flowing.

This is a critical element in learning to dream again, because we have a natural tendency to settle for good rather than strive for great. In seeking His blessings, it's easy for us to feel satisfied with "enough" when we could have "abundance."

For example, imagine if the widow had been keeping track of those jars and thought, *This is enough to pay off my creditors, so I'll stop pouring. I don't want to push this miracle too far.* She would have missed so much of the blessing God intended for her!

Let God do the heavy lifting for your dreams. Let Him keep pouring until He chooses to stop, because His fruitfulness will always exceed our faithfulness.

On a practical level, if you have a God-sized dream to find a spouse, then chase the absolute best spouse in the world! Don't settle for someone who is "good enough." Don't settle for someone who feels comfortable or nice or safe. Instead, keep chasing that dream until God pours out every drop—until

He brings you the person who fills you with joy and life and laughter and a deep, genuine love.

If you have a God-sized dream to start a specific career, then put in the time to research the very best job available with the very best company. Don't limit yourself based on what you feel qualified for, because God has no limits! And rather than applying to one or two good jobs, send out ten applications. Set out ten jars and see how many God chooses to fill. He just may astound you with His grace and generosity!

DON'T LIMIT YOURSELF BASED ON WHAT YOU FEEL QUALIFIED FOR, BECAUSE GOD HAS NO LIMITS!

If you have a message burning in your heart, get out there and find the people who need to hear it. Start a blog. Create a YouTube channel. Look for opportunities to speak in your community or in churches and schools close by. Do everything in your power to share that message faithfully, and give God every opportunity to amplify it through *His* megaphone.

Again, follow the instructions He gives you. Set out the jars according to His leading—but let Him do the heavy lifting to fill those jars.

When I started Next Level Church, I received a subscription to *Outreach* magazine, which is written largely for pastors and church leaders. Each year, *Outreach* puts out a special edition that tracks the "100 Fastest Growing Churches in America." I kept that magazine on my desk when we launched in 2008, and I dreamed of one day seeing our church on that list.

My dream wasn't about the numbers. Instead, I thought it

would be so awesome to have a church show up on that list that was located in the least-churched region in the country. I was charged up at the idea of Jesus doing something in our part of the world that so many people said could never be done.

Sure enough, in 2014, NLC was number five on that list. We've seen God do the impossible!

Similarly, I can remember dreaming during the early days of NLC that we would see five hundred people worshiping together in our community. But when we hit that goal, we didn't stop dreaming; we didn't put any limits on what God could do. We just kept setting out jars as quickly as we could. And at a recent Easter service, we saw more than nine thousand people join together in worship across our different campuses.

In case I haven't made it clear already, God is the one who has done the heavy lifting at Next Level Church. We've got a great staff and great volunteers, and we all work hard. But we could never accomplish what we've seen. Just like the widow in 2 Kings 4, we've been blessed by our generous, gracious, all-powerful God, and He wants to bless you as well!

I don't know what's on the outside of your LEGO box. I don't know what dreams God has planted in your heart. I don't know what your hopes for the future are. But if you're ready to dream again, I'm confident that the same God who turned a little bit of oil into more than enough for an overwhelmed widow can take what you bring to the table and turn it into abundance. He can fill your life with grace upon grace.

Are you ready?

AS WE MOVE
STEP-BY-STEP IN
FAITHFULNESS, GOD
STAYS WITH US
AND CONTINUES TO
GUIDE US TOWARD
THE GOAL.

six

ENEMIES, ENCOURAGERS, AND EXPERTS—OH MY!

Surround yourself with only people who are going to lift you higher.

—OPRAH WINFREY

"You're five feet nothin', 100 and nothin', and you got hardly a speck of athletic ability. And you hung in with the best college football team in the land for two years. And you're also gonna walk outta here with a degree from the University of Notre Dame. In this lifetime, you don't have to prove nothin' to nobody except yourself."[1]

Do you recognize that quote? It's from the movie *Rudy*, which is one of my all-time favorite films. And let me say, *man*, I get fired up even just reading that line. It's so inspiring!

Rudy is a biographical sports film based on a University of Notre Dame student named Rudy Ruettiger. From the time he was a little boy, Rudy had a dream to play football as part of the UND Fighting Irish. But because he was small in stature and struggled with academics, he wasn't an obvious fit for the team. In fact, nobody gave a serious thought to Rudy's dream coming true.

Except Rudy.

Growing up, Rudy's home life was difficult. He had a rocky relationship with his family, including his father, Daniel, and his older brother, Frank. Both Daniel and Frank repeatedly told Rudy that his dream to play football at Notre Dame was ridiculous and that he was destined to spend his life working in the local steel mill, just like every other man in their family. They hammered those opinions into Rudy's mind and heart over and over again—until he finally accepted their words as his identity, gave up his dream, and settled for the life everyone else desired for him.

Everything seemed hopeless for Rudy as he carried the weight of a dream that felt dead on his shoulders, until he had an eye-opening conversation with his friend Pete on Rudy's twenty-second birthday. In one of my favorite scenes from the movie, Pete gives Rudy a Notre Dame letterman jacket as a birthday gift during their lunch break at the steel mill. Filled with awe, Rudy symbolically covers his steel-workers' uniform with the new jacket.

That's the moment you can see a pulse begin to beat once again for Rudy's dream. His hope wasn't dead after all—just lingering below the surface and waiting for something to jolt it back to life. (See why I like this movie so much?)

In that scene, Rudy looks at his friend and says, "You're the only one who ever took me serious, Pete."

Pete's answer is critical: "Well, you know what my dad always said: having dreams is what makes life tolerable." Ultimately, Pete's belief in Rudy is what compelled him to chase and eventually achieve his dream of playing football at Notre Dame.

I've learned that we will encounter lots of Franks and very few Petes in life. And not only will the Franks always seem greater in number, they will also be louder in volume. As a result, we have to be careful which voices we allow to influence our decisions and our futures, lest we become the clone of everyone else's opinion and cover over the masterpiece God designed.

The fastest way to forget what God thinks of you is to become consumed by what the Franks of this world think of you.

So let me ask you: Who are you going to trust with your dreams? Who are you going to share them with? Who are you going to seek help from when you need a boost? Who are you going to listen to and allow to influence you as you chase your God-inspired, God-sized future? That's the core theme of this chapter.

> **THE FASTEST WAY TO FORGET WHAT GOD THINKS OF YOU IS TO BECOME CONSUMED BY WHAT THE FRANKS OF THIS WORLD THINK OF YOU.**

In the pages that follow, we're going to explore three different types of relationships that often influence the way we move forward: enemies, encouragers, and experts.

Understanding the dynamics of these relationships will help you surround yourself with people who stand beside you, speak truthfully, and motivate you to pursue your God-sized dreams.

ENEMIES

I know, *enemy* is such a harsh word. Nobody likes to think of themselves as having enemies, especially normal, run-of-the-mill folks like you and me.

But I use the word *enemies* here intentionally, because it's important for us to understand that there really are people out there who are willing to harm you. The people who fit into this category typically aren't our personal enemies who want to destroy us—they're not a nemesis like Lex Luthor is for Superman.

No, such people are the enemies of our dreams. For a number of reasons, they want us to quit striving for greatness, give up on our dearest hopes, and settle for safe and comfortable dreams—along with safe and comfortable lives—that are utterly unremarkable.

Obviously, removing ourselves from the influence of such people is an important part of pursuing our God-sized dreams. But how do we identify those who are the enemies of our dreams? What do they look like and how do they attempt to derail us?

Let's explore the two most common forms of people who set themselves up as enemies of our dreams. I call them zombies and vampires.

Zombies

First of all, let me make it clear that zombies are not real. They are fictional monsters, and I don't want to give anyone the impression that I believe zombies are actually walking around somewhere in the world today. Because if I did believe that, I would probably have to live in one of those underground bunkers for the rest of my life. But zombies have received a lot of attention through movies and television in recent years, which makes them an effective illustration.

What do we know about zombies? Number one, they are destructive. They don't care about anything except attacking and eating and smashing whatever gets in their path. Number two, they are fundamentally opposed to life and joy and happiness. What a zombie wants most is to make the rest of the world like itself—uncaring and unfeeling and motivated by consumption. So whenever a zombie sees anything alive or bright or exceptional, it tries to kill it. To consume it. To turn it into just another zombie.

In our lives, zombies are those people who try to drag us down to their level. They push us to cross boundaries—to watch things we wouldn't normally watch, say things we wouldn't normally say, and do things we wouldn't normally do. It's the adult who tries to expose younger people to pornography. It's the coworker who is overly flirtatious. It's the older sibling who constantly reminds us that we're not good enough, smart enough, and talented enough to fulfill our dreams.

Maybe you're wondering, *How are zombies different from the garden-variety bad influences that pop up in our lives?*

Well, there's not much difference except for one important fact: zombies are those we stay close to—those we interact with on a regular basis—which means they are those we allow to have access to our dreams. Whether they are family or they have some other official connection in our lives, zombies are difficult to avoid.

But we must avoid them. Proverbs 13:20 says, "Walk with the wise and become wise; associate with fools and get in trouble." And 1 Corinthians 15:33 says, "Don't be fooled by those who say such things, for 'bad company corrupts good character.'" If we allow ourselves to be influenced by zombies, we shouldn't be surprised when our lives head down paths we never intended to travel.

Zombies are especially dangerous because they love to target our dreams. Typically, people who qualify as zombies have a pretty good understanding that their lives have not turned out the way they hoped. They feel disappointed and dissatisfied. But rather than try to renew a spark of life in their own dreams, they find pleasure in extinguishing that spark in the dreams of others. They want to make everyone like themselves so that they don't feel as bad about their own failures.

Who are the relational zombies in your life? Who are the ones who always seem to pull you down—to pull you away from God's plan and purpose for your life?

Once you identify those people, it's time to build some healthy boundaries. Put some distance between you and them. Remove their influence from your life and especially from your God-sized dreams.

Vampires

The second type of enemy I want to discuss are vampires (also fictional). Like zombies, vampires are harmful influences who threaten our dreams. Unlike zombies, however, vampires are much more subtle and much less obvious. And where zombies do nothing but bring death and destruction, vampires are more interested in slowly sucking the life out of us.

Recently, I heard NBA broadcaster Ernie Johnson talking about America's strained political climate. He said that instead of participating in the frequent negative discourse, he had chosen to be part of the solution. He stated, "I have to look in the mirror and say, 'How am I going to be a better man? How am I going to be a better neighbor? How am I going to be a better citizen? How am I going to be a better American? How can I be a fountain and not a drain?'"[2]

The last question stands out to me because it's a great way to think about vampires. To put it simply, the vampires in our lives are drains. They constantly take rather than give. For my part, I want to be a fountain who gives life to those around me, and I want to spend my time with fountains, not drains.

In Proverbs 18:21, Solomon warned us of the power and influence of words: "The tongue can bring death or life; those who love to talk will reap the consequences." Vampires often use words to bring death to those they are around. They are the people who always seem negative and miserable. They complain about everything. If they win the lottery, they complain about having to pay taxes on their winnings. They say things like "You will never" or "It will never" or "You don't know how." They're gossips who are consistently critical and judgmental.

At the same time, vampires are subtle in their influence. They aren't typically mean people who don't get along with anyone; it's usually the opposite. They are good people who are emotionally immature.

Finally, vampires have a unique ability to bring to life the insecurities you're already battling. Whatever pain, drama, or challenge you have managed to keep lingering just below the surface, they find a way to dig it up and expose it. In fact, they love to dig for areas of pain in your life and then poke at them—sometimes just for the fun of seeing how you'll react.

On a practical level, a vampire is that friend who always leaves you feeling kind of down after a conversation. It's the relative who has a way of consistently pointing out the flaws in your plans, or the neighbor who regularly wants to engage you in a conversation about whose kids are misbehaving down the street.

Whereas zombies will try to kill your dreams because they are afraid of them, vampires will try to drain your time and your energy and your joy as you pursue those dreams. Both need to be avoided at all costs.

ENCOURAGERS

As I've mentioned, it's critical to remove enemies from your life as you begin the process of chasing your dreams. But that doesn't mean you can or should chase a God-sized dream on your own.

Far from it! You need people who can help and support you on the journey, and you need people who can bring strength and energy and wisdom into your life when the going gets tough.

I call such people encouragers, and there are two types in this category I want us to focus on: sidekicks and heroes.

Sidekicks

"Holy zeppelin!" "Holy birthday cake!" "Holy headache!" "Holy smoke!" What do these phrases have in common? They are just a few of the many exclamations used by Batman's trusty sidekick, Robin. Sure, Robin may not be as cool or as tough as Batman, and his suit leaves much to be desired. But he's a true friend and a critical part of the Caped Crusader's crime-fighting success.

We all need a Robin by our side—someone reliable who will fight with us to defeat the villains who come our way. The Bible describes the role of a Robin, or what I like to call a sidekick, this way: "As iron sharpens iron, so a friend sharpens a friend" (Prov. 27:17).

A few years ago I went horseback riding at the Lost Valley Dude Ranch in Colorado. During our ride through the Colorado mountains, I learned an interesting fact about draft horses. Each of these massive, muscular animals is strong enough to pull up to 8,000 pounds—but when two of them are teamed up, together they can pull up to 24,000 pounds. What's more, when the two horses have trained together and have synergy, they can pull up to 32,000 pounds in tandem!

In a similar way, our ability to pursue our dreams can receive a massive boost when we team up with people who have invested in our lives and are willing to join up and help pull the load. And when you find someone who really gets what you are trying to accomplish and puts their full weight behind you—when you find a Pete, for example—the boost is exponential.

The power of unity is illustrated in Ecclesiastes 4:9–10: "Two people are better off than one, for they can help each other succeed. If one person falls, the other can reach out and help. But someone who falls alone is in real trouble."

We all need sidekicks in our lives. These are people who believe in our dreams and with whom we share a common purpose. They see our potential, speak life into our situations, and challenge us to grow. Sidekicks aren't yes-men. They don't always tell us what we want to hear, but they encourage us to become a better version of ourselves.

I have a handful of sidekicks who supported me during the launch of NLC and who continue to support me as we keep striving for new levels in this God-sized dream. Those sidekicks include my wife, Jennifer, my executive team at Next Level Church, and others that I've trusted to be in my inner circle. Each of these people has the authority to protect, encourage, correct, and guide me into becoming the man that God desires for me to become. I've given them that authority because they earned it by proving themselves over and over.

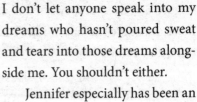

I DON'T LET ANYONE SPEAK INTO MY DREAMS WHO HASN'T POURED SWEAT AND TEARS INTO THOSE DREAMS ALONGSIDE ME. YOU SHOULDN'T EITHER.

Remember what I said earlier: I don't let anyone speak into my dreams who hasn't poured sweat and tears into those dreams alongside me. You shouldn't either.

Jennifer especially has been an incredible support for me. There were times when I was ready to give up our dream of planting a church, largely because that dream drained so much of our finances and seemed as if it would cause harm to our family. But each time

I got ready to throw in the towel, Jennifer was there beside me to say, "God is behind this. God will provide what we need. We trust Him and we trust you."

I'll never be able to express how meaningful those moments have been in my journey!

Who are the Robins in your life? Who stands beside you in battle and reminds you that you're not a failure? Do you have someone who supports your God-given dreams? Just as Rudy needed his friend Pete, and Batman will always rely on Robin, you need people in your life who help you pull more weight than you ever could pull alone.

Heroes

Whereas sidekicks walk beside us, heroes go before us. They are the examples we follow. Heroes are people we admire because they are living the kind of life we desire.

For example, I have the privilege of regularly spending time with an eighty-year-old man I admire deeply. He has opened up his life and heart to me, and I gain wisdom and understanding from hearing about his experiences. He's been in the ministry for decades and has stood on some of the world's most influential platforms. However, despite his wealth of ministerial knowledge, we rarely spend time talking about ministry; instead, we spend hours discussing the importance of living our lives with purpose.

It's been said that "everyone will end up somewhere, but not everyone gets there on purpose." I like that. And I want the time I spend with my hero to help me end up somewhere on purpose. I don't want to be so focused on the here and now that I fail to protect the things that matter most in life. So, instead of asking my friend questions about how to grow a church, I ask him what he is learning from Jesus, how he connects with God and hears His voice, how he has raised children of integrity, and what it takes to stay in love and remain faithful to the same woman for more than fifty years.

The last time I saw this hero, he said: "The older I get, Josh, the more I realize that our time on earth is coming to an end. My wife and I are both old, and she's aging faster than I am." As his eyes watered, he continued, "Every morning I wake up and hold her tighter than the day before because I'm unsure how many mornings we have left together."

We both choked back tears and sat in silence, feeling the weight of that moment. And I thought, *That's why I love this man so much. He's winning in the areas of life that are most important.* I hope I can do the same.

Heroes are people living their current lives in our desired tomorrow. They are accomplishing what we hope to someday accomplish. Heroes serve as targets for us to aim our lives at. That's important, because we'll never arrive at our desired destination if we are unclear of where the bull's-eye is.

Having heroes allows us to aim our lives at our desired outcomes. If you dream of having a great marriage, you need to find a hero whose successful marriage can serve as a model for yours. If you long to beat an addiction, you need to find a hero who has broken its stronghold. If you want to start a business, you need a hero who can teach you the ropes. If you have a dream to raise kids of integrity, find a hero who has raised children who love God and are happy and respectful. If you're in a financial stranglehold, you need a hero who can show you the way to financial freedom.

In short, if you have a dream to _____, you need to find a hero who has successfully _____. How would you fill in those blanks?

What I'm really talking about in this hero/follower relationship is mentorship. Or, to use a more spiritual word, discipleship. Mentorship is a thoroughly biblical principle, and it would take several pages to list the mentor relationships in Scripture. But just to name a few, Moses was a mentor to Joshua, Jesus was a mentor to His disciples, and the apostle Paul mentored Timothy and Titus. Paul also wrote many letters to the churches he planted, encouraging them to follow Jesus' example and teaching them what they needed to know.

Listen to the advice the apostle Paul gave the church in Philippi, for example: "Keep putting into practice all you learned and received from me—everything you heard from me and saw me doing. Then the God of peace will be with you" (Phil. 4:9).

There's no better way to end up where you want to be than to spend time with people who can show you how to get there. That's why everyone needs heroes in their lives, especially as they pursue their God-sized dreams.

But don't overlook one important thing: you have an opportunity not only to find a hero but to *be* a hero. That's right! You've accomplished noteworthy things in your life, and you'll accomplish more as you pursue your God-sized dreams. Therefore, you are (or will be) in a place to help and support others coming behind you who are looking for a hero. Everyone should have a hero helping them get somewhere on purpose, and everyone should be a hero guiding someone somewhere on purpose.

EXPERTS

We've covered two types of relationships that have influence over our dreams, and it's easy to see where each of them fall. Enemies are bad and cause harm to our dreams, while encouragers are good and help us achieve them. The categories are obvious.

But things are different for the third group of relationships, which I refer to as experts. That's because experts can both help us and harm us as we pursue our dreams—which means we need to be wise in how to approach them and allow them to speak into our lives.

First, what do I mean by experts? Simply put, an expert is someone who has authority, experience, and wisdom in a specific area or field. For example, I've always been impressed with people who, unlike myself, can fix their own vehicles. I'm no mechanic, and I'm clueless when it comes to anything with an engine. As embarrassing as it is, I only recently learned that when changing a tire, you should loosen the lug nuts before jacking up the vehicle. (If you didn't know that either, then consider yourself my first auto mechanic student!)

So, obviously, a mechanic is an expert when it comes to fixing cars. But there are experts on every subject imaginable—people who have authority, experience, and wisdom in those subjects. There are marriage experts. There are Bible experts. There are gardening experts and golf experts and financial experts.

In this way, experts are similar to heroes in that they can help us find a target for our lives, and they can give us information to help us reach our goals. If you have a God-sized dream to launch a specific career, then it's probably a good idea to speak with an expert in that career or field. If your dream is to break free from an addiction, you may want to speak with someone who is an expert at helping people do exactly that.

Experts can provide a lot of value and a lot of help as we pursue our dreams.

However, there's a big difference between experts and heroes. Namely, an expert is someone who has information but no relationship. Experts have facts, but they rarely understand your story and they have not invested in your pursuit of your dreams. They are outside observers.

For that reason, we need to be cautious about how much influence we allow experts to have over our dreams. I had several church-planting experts, for example, who told me it was hopeless to plant a new church in New England. They told me my dreams could never come true—that was their expert opinion, and they were expertly wrong.

Similarly, a scientific expert would have told Peter that it's impossible to walk on water, and shared with Mary and Martha that it's impossible for Lazarus to come back to life.

There's another example in the Bible of how expert opinions almost prevented an entire nation from walking into God's blessing. The book of Numbers tells the story of God's chosen people, the Israelites, as they journeyed through the desert in search of the promised land. After months of traveling, they finally reached their destination, and we can only imagine how overwhelmed with emotion they must have been as they stood along its border. They had finally arrived!

Before stepping into their promise, the Lord told Moses to send out some volunteers to explore the land:

"Send out men to explore the land of Canaan, the land I am giving to the Israelites. Send one leader from each of the twelve ancestral tribes." So Moses did as the LORD commanded him. He sent out twelve men, all tribal leaders of Israel, from their camp in the wilderness of Paran. (Num. 13:1–3)

Unfortunately, Moses sent out men who were experts at evaluating land and fighting wars—not experts on what God had already done and had promised to do in the future. So, after exploring the promised land for forty days, the twelve scouts came back and shared their opinions with Moses and the Israelites:

"We entered the land you sent us to explore, and it is indeed a bountiful country—a land flowing with milk and honey. Here is the kind of fruit it produces. But the people living there are powerful, and their towns are large and fortified. We even saw giants there, the descendants of Anak! The Amalekites live in the Negev, and the Hittites, Jebusites, and Amorites live in the hill country. The Canaanites live along the coast of the Mediterranean Sea and along the Jordan Valley."

But Caleb tried to quiet the people as they stood before Moses. "Let's go at once to take the land," he said. "We can certainly conquer it!"

But the other men who had explored the land with him disagreed. "We can't go up against them! They are stronger than we are!" So they spread this bad report about the land among the Israelites: "The land we traveled through and explored will devour anyone who goes to live there. All the people we saw were huge. We even saw giants there, the descendants of Anak. Next to them we felt like grasshoppers, and that's what they thought, too!" (13:27–33)

Of the twelve experts sent into the promised land, ten returned with a negative report. And those ten persuaded the entire nation to believe that their dream of receiving the promised land was impossible. They convinced the Israelites to see themselves as grasshoppers in a giant's world.

As a result, the Israelites wandered in the desert for forty years. During those four decades, an entire generation missed out on their dream, their miracle, and their God-given promise because they allowed the opinions of "experts" to convince them that there was no hope.

In today's world, I don't want to see a couple give up on their dream of healing their relationship because a marriage counselor—an expert—says it is impossible. I don't want someone with cancer or another illness to stop praying and believing God for healing because a doctor says there's no hope, just six more weeks to live.

In short, don't be afraid to seek counsel from experts. Use their experience and their authority to help you gain as much information as possible. On the other hand, *do* be very cautious about letting an expert talk you out of your dream. Experts see what's possible through a human understanding— but there's always more that can be accomplished when God enters the equation. Even the impossible.

As you pick up the pace on your journey of pursuing your dreams, you will encounter zombies, vampires, sidekicks, heroes, and experts. You will have opportunities to allow each of these relationships to be present in one form or another in your life, which means you must choose whether and how much each one is able to influence your dreams.

Choose wisely!

THERE'S NO BETTER WAY
TO END UP WHERE YOU
WANT TO BE THAN TO
SPEND TIME WITH PEOPLE
WHO CAN SHOW YOU
HOW TO GET THERE.

seven

DANGEROUS PRAYERS

To be a Christian without prayer is no more possible than
to be alive without breathing.

—MARTIN LUTHER[1]

The phone woke me out of a deep sleep. It was early on the
morning of September 22, and when I looked at the name on
my phone screen, I smiled. My friends Daniel and Katherine
were expecting the birth of their first baby, and I knew
Katherine had gone into labor the night before. I was hoping
and expecting to hear good news.

But as soon as I heard Daniel's voice on the other end of
the line, I knew something was wrong. Very wrong.

"Hi, Pastor," he said. "Josiah was born, but there are more
health issues than we'd been expecting."

I told him I'd head to the hospital right away.

Daniel and Katherine had known their son had some health issues. At one point during Katherine's pregnancy, her doctor informed them that one of Josiah's kidneys had ruptured, and the medical team wasn't sure if the non-ruptured kidney was functioning as it should. As a church, we began to pray regularly for Josiah, and we believed that God would heal him. But based on my brief conversation with Daniel, that prayer had not been answered in the way we hoped.

When I arrived at the hospital, Daniel confirmed the worst: Josiah's kidney failure was only one of many health problems the doctors discovered after he was born. I didn't know what to say, so I prayed, I cried, and I did my best to encourage this beautiful family.

Out of respect for their family, I won't provide you with an extensive list of Josiah's health problems. But I can tell you that he endured nine major surgeries in the first year of his life, and he spent more nights in the hospital than he did at home. Today, Josiah is ten years old, and he's had over thirty surgeries.

Despite the many trials he's faced, Josiah is an awesome kid. He's supersmart and uncommonly witty, and he loves Jesus. Looking at him, you would never know the challenges he faces each day—and you'd never guess that, outside of a miracle, he will face those challenges and more for the rest of his life.

Recently, Jennifer and I had dinner with Daniel and Katherine. During the meal, we reflected on the last decade of doing life together. I asked Katherine, "What's been the hardest part of the last ten years?" (Of course, I meant outside of watching her baby go through hell.)

Katherine's eyes filled with tears before she answered, "Praying." Silence fell over the table until, with tears now rolling down her cheeks, she continued: "When I was pregnant with Josiah, I prayed every day that God would heal him, and I believed that He would. When he was born and my miracle prayer hadn't been answered, I continued to pray. I prayed and prayed and prayed. With everything in me, I prayed and believed that God would heal my baby. Now, ten years later, I still pray, but it's not the same. I miss the way I used to pray. The boldness. The passion. The belief that God would move on my behalf, that my dream of seeing my son healed would come true."

We were all silent as we cried with her. After a few more minutes, Katherine smiled through the tears and said, "Pastor Josh, you always ask the worst questions at dinner!"

We all laughed. We forced ourselves to continue eating, and eventually things returned to a more normal social atmosphere. But the weight of that conversation and the rawness of Katherine's honesty still shakes me to my core.

As Jennifer and I drove home from dinner that evening, I tried to describe the impact our conversation with Daniel and Katherine had on me. For the first time, I realized that our prayers and our dreams are not two separate expressions of who we are. Instead, they are directly connected. When our ability to dream becomes weak, the same happens to our prayer life. And vice versa.

I realized that our prayers are often conversations with God about our dreams.

Many people believe they have a problem with prayer, and rightfully so. But I think our issues with prayer go

> **WHEN OUR ABILITY TO DREAM BECOMES WEAK, THE SAME HAPPENS TO OUR PRAYER LIFE.**

deeper—I think they start as a dream problem. Our dream life intersects with our prayer life; they're connected. As a result, big and bold dreams lead to big and bold prayers, which is fantastic. However, when we feel wounded by unfulfilled dreams, we tend to retreat into a shell where we only allow ourselves safe and comfortable dreams. Which means we settle for safe and comfortable prayers.

Think back to a time when you believed your dreams and hopes for tomorrow were just around the corner. Was there more passion in your prayer life? More faith? More boldness? I bet there was. Why? Because our dream life inspires our prayer life. In fact, if you were to sit down with me and tell me about your dreams, I feel confident I could describe your prayer life pretty accurately. They're connected that strongly.

In the weeks after my dinner conversation with Daniel and Katherine, I wrestled with several key questions about this connection between our prayers and our dreams. *How do we overcome our problems with prayer? How do we continue to pray when our dreams seem dead? How do we pray even when it feels as if God doesn't care? How do we continue to pray with faith even when our desired future doesn't become a living reality?*

In this chapter, I'll work through the results of that wrestling and share what I've learned. This is important for a few reasons. First and foremost, prayer is a critical part of following God, and if you've been living with a dream that's been buried or presumed dead, that reality has affected your prayer life. As I said above, when our dreams die, so do our prayers.

Second, if you're starting to let go of disappointment and learning to dream again—and I sincerely hope you are—then you'll need prayer. You'll need a constant connection with the

Source and Supporter of your dreams. That's because prayer is to a follower of Christ what oxygen is to a marathon runner.

As you move forward with chasing your dreams, it's critical for you to restore your intimacy with God and experience His wisdom, strength, encouragement, and guidance.

RESTORING THE CONNECTION

I love the way my sons pray. Their prayers are big, bold, and unstained by disappointment. In fact, my boys prayed over you and me before I sat down to write this chapter. They prayed that God would give me wisdom and that everyone who reads this book would be encouraged to believe their best days truly are still ahead. I'm amazed at their confidence—they're so certain that God is listening!

It's hard for us to pray that way when we're carrying the weight of unanswered prayers—especially when those unanswered prayers extend over a lifetime. It's hard for us to really pray in faith when we've seen dreams die on the vine and felt the sting of no after no.

That's why many of us today are living with a prayer problem: a lie that we believe to be truth will affect our lives as if it were true. Therefore, if we live each day believing that God doesn't hear our prayers, doesn't care about our dreams, and doesn't give us the strength we need to pursue a better tomorrow, we'll start living as if those falsehoods are actually true. We'll find ourselves becoming more and more distant from God and missing out on the intimate relationship He desires to share with us.

This is a problem we need to fix before we'll have a realistic chance of pursuing our God-sized dreams with hope and confidence.

I'm going to say something here that may sound frustrating, but hear me out: prayer is the only antidote to our problems with praying. That's because prayer is the only way for us to restore intimacy with God.

There are two ways to fight within a marriage: you can fight fair and you can fight dirty. I always teach married couples that fighting is inevitable, but how you fight will determine the health of your marriage. When Jennifer and I first got married, we fought dirty. She yelled at me, and I threw things. The louder she got, the more pillows, shoes, or remote controls I sent flying. (Thankfully, I never threw anything at Jennifer or even in her direction; otherwise, she would have kicked my butt.)

Whenever we finished one of our unfair fights, Jennifer would want to sit down and talk through things—try to process what happened and how we could fix it. But not me. I pretended the argument never happened, and I allowed anger and bitterness to fester inside me.

A year into our marriage, I realized that my lack of communication was blocking intimacy in our relationship. Jennifer and I were drifting apart. It wasn't the arguments that were the problem. It was my unwillingness to communicate my way through the pain. After one argument, when I was reluctant to talk, Jennifer said, "If all you want is a roommate for the rest of your life, then that's what I'll be. But that's not what I want. I want to be your wife, and I want to know how you feel and I want to be able to tell you how I feel. The only way for us to move forward in health is to communicate our way toward intimacy."

I acted as though those words didn't knock the air out of my lungs, but they did. I realized that the only way I could build and maintain an intimate relationship with Jennifer was to talk through the pain. Communication is the only way to ensure intimacy. Today, because we choose to fight fair and communicate even when it's easier to remain silent, Jennifer is not only my wife, but she's also my bestie—my ride or die.

There's a similar dynamic at play in our relationship with God. Namely, the only way for us to increase our intimacy with God is by talking with Him. We have to be willing to fight fair and tell God how we feel. We have to pray even when we don't feel like praying, even when we're not exactly sure what to say, and even when it feels as if our prayers are not being heard.

> WE HAVE TO PRAY EVEN WHEN WE DON'T FEEL LIKE PRAYING, EVEN WHEN WE'RE NOT EXACTLY SURE WHAT TO SAY, AND EVEN WHEN IT FEELS AS IF OUR PRAYERS ARE NOT BEING HEARD.

Many of us who grew up in church have been taught—both directly and indirectly—that God isn't interested in the real us: the broken us, the doubting us, and the us who wants to give up sometimes. But that's a lie! God wants to connect with the real you in real ways; He's not interested in a fake relationship any more than you are.

That's why there are moments in the Bible like this:

> O Lord, you misled me,
>> and I allowed myself to be misled.
> You are stronger than I am,
>> and you overpowered me.
> Now I am mocked every day;
>> everyone laughs at me. (Jer. 20:7)

Those words were written by a prophet named Jeremiah. He was one of God's spokespersons in the Old Testament, charged with declaring God's message to His people. Unfortunately for Jeremiah, God's people didn't really want to hear it, and they made his life miserable for years. Not surprisingly, there are several moments in the book of Jeremiah where the prophet expressed confusion, anger, and even accusations of unfairness toward God.

And you know what? God apparently handled it okay. All of it. He allowed Jeremiah to express himself openly and honestly, and He never once zapped him with a lightning bolt. He even allowed Jeremiah's complaints to become part of the Bible! So I think it's fair to say that God can handle our emotions, including frustration.

God wants a genuine, intimate relationship with you. And you need a genuine, intimate relationship with God if you want to pursue and achieve your God-sized dreams. Restore the lines of communication with God. Knock off the rust and break out of those ruts—reject the safe and comfortable prayers you've allowed yourself to settle for over the years.

Remember: the only way to fix a prayer problem is to pray. To help you get started, let's walk through three ice-breaking prayers you can add to your life that will help you reconnect with God and increase the intimacy of your connection to Him.

1. GOD, HELP ME TRUST YOUR CHARACTER OVER MY CIRCUMSTANCES

As I mentioned earlier, prayer is communication with God—nothing more and nothing less. But in order for your communication to be as meaningful as possible, it helps to have a firm understanding of the One with whom you're communicating.

It's helpful to understand God's character—who He is and what He values. And the easiest way for us to examine God's character up close is to take a look at the life and ministry of Jesus in the Scriptures. As you examine Jesus' reality as God in the flesh and explore His interactions with others, you'll get a clearer picture of God's character.

It is evident in Scripture that Jesus loved those who were seen as unlovable, showed compassion to broken people *and* the religious leaders who wanted to stone Him, invited the most wretched sinners in the town to walk with Him, offered forgiveness to those who rejected Him, and healed the overlooked from their diseases. This helps us understand that God's character is loyal, loving, all-knowing, all-powerful, righteous, just, true, graceful, hopeful, and helpful. (That's just the beginning, of course. Anything I could say about God will always fall short of His majesty, brilliance, and beauty—His holiness.)

Here's the problem: most of us allow the day-to-day circumstances of our lives to form our understanding of who God is and what He values. We allow our experiences to shape what we believe about His character. That's how we start to think of God as a Cosmic Vending Machine who exists only to grant our wishes, or as a Divine Accountant who spends His days constantly checking over our thoughts and actions in search of mistakes to punish.

When that happens, however, we're not worshiping or praying to the God of the Bible. We're trying to connect with an idol we've chosen to call God—which of course won't work very well, because idols never answer our prayers.

Horatio G. Spafford is a beautiful example of someone who didn't allow his circumstances to form his understanding of God's character. Spafford was born into a Presbyterian family in Chicago in 1828 and grew up to be a successful lawyer and follower of Jesus, counting American evangelist Dwight L. Moody as one of his closest friends. Beginning in 1871, a series of extraordinarily unfortunate events struck Spafford's family. It started with the death of his son, continued with the destruction of nearly everything he owned in the Great Chicago Fire, and culminated in the death of his four daughters when their ship, bound for a family vacation in Europe, sunk while crossing the ocean.

When he received word of the shipwreck and the death of his daughters, Spafford immediately boarded a ship to Europe to be with his wife. While sailing across the ocean, Spafford penned the now-famous hymn "It Is Well with My Soul." As he neared the area where his daughters had perished, he wrote the following:

> When peace, like a river, attendeth my way,
> When sorrows like sea billows roll;
> Whatever my lot, thou hast taught me to say,
> It is well, it is well with my soul.

I can't help but fight back tears each time I read these words or sing that beautiful hymn. Was Spafford happy about what happened? Of course not! But he found peace in knowing that if the character of God is good and perfect, then His plan must be as well. Secure in that knowledge, Spafford and his wife continued to chase their dreams despite continued tragedy. They had more children, lost another son, and finished their days doing missionary and humanitarian work in Jerusalem.[2]

The circumstances in our lives are constantly changing—constantly moving up and down. But God never changes. He is the same yesterday, today, and forever.

Therefore, you can use God's unchanging nature as a foundation for your prayer life. As you seek to restore the intimacy in your connection with Him, start this way: "God, please help me trust Your character over my circumstances."

I've also found it helpful to talk with God about what I'm learning of His character or how His character has been confirmed through my experiences. "God, I know You are good, and I proclaim Your goodness even though I'm feeling frustrated right now." Or "Lord, Your Word says You are faithful, and I can see how You are faithfully opening doors right now as I pursue this dream. Thank You, Lord God, for Your faithfulness."

2. GOD, HELP ME SEE POSSIBILITIES WHEN I'M SURROUNDED BY IMPOSSIBILITIES

If you're an NBA fan, you've probably heard of former professional basketball player Kevin Garnett. In his thirteenth season as a professional, Garnett won his first NBA championship.

Can you imagine waiting thirteen years for a dream like that? Selfishly, I'm happy his dream came true while he was playing for my favorite team, the Boston Celtics. (Go Celtics!)

There is a powerful video clip from a moment during Garnett's postgame interview. As confetti was falling around him, Garnett looked at the camera and yelled, "Anything is possible!" You need to watch the clip if you haven't seen it, because those words came out with every ounce of his being. It was a passionate explosion of joy and a thrilling reminder that dreams can finally come true.

This world is a tough place, and circumstances often play out differently than we hope or expect. Sometimes it seems as if we are surrounded by impossibilities. By long odds and little hope. In those moments, we as followers of Christ need to shout out the truth that anything is possible! We need to regularly remind ourselves that nothing is impossible for God. Nothing!

There's a dad in the book of Matthew who understood this reality. He ran up to Jesus in need of a miracle, and he believed that nothing is impossible for God. Jesus was in the middle of a conversation about fasting when the guy interrupted Him:

As Jesus was saying this, the leader of a synagogue came and knelt before him. "My daughter has just died," he said, "but you can bring her back to life again if you just come and lay your hand on her." (Matt. 9:18)

As a father myself, I can feel the emotion behind this man's desperate plea. I picture him looking up at Jesus, his body shaking, his lungs fighting for oxygen after his long sprint to find the Healer. I envision tears in his eyes as he begs Jesus to bring his daughter, his dream, back to life.

Don't miss the truth that this man came looking for a miracle. He thought his dream, his future, and his hopes were quite literally dead, which means he had a choice. He could have pulled back from God in that moment and retreated toward bitterness, despair, and anger. Instead, he went directly to the one person he believed could turn his impossibilities into possibilities.

The Bible tells us what happened next:

> When Jesus arrived at the official's home, he saw the noisy crowd and heard the funeral music. "Get out!" he told them. "The girl isn't dead; she's only asleep." But the crowd laughed at him. After the crowd was put outside, however, Jesus went in and took the girl by the hand, and she stood up! (vv. 23–25)

Do you know why the crowd laughed? It's because they could see only the impossibilities in the situation. They saw the dead girl, and based on their own eyes and their past experiences, they knew she would never come back to life.

The father was different. I can imagine him bouncing on his tiptoes with excitement because *Jesus was in the house.* And when Jesus is in the house, *anything is possible!*

I want to live like that dad did. I don't want to go through each day laughing in sarcasm at the impossibilities of my circumstances. I want to believe that God is God over my circumstances. Now, I'm not saying nothing ever dies—there are real tragedies in this world, and we have to trust God's character in the midst of that pain. But we often give up on our dreams because we forget that when Jesus shows up, nothing is impossible. Anything can happen.

I believe that God still heals the sick, comforts the hurting, gives strength to the weak, and brings dead things back to life. That's why a big part of my prayer life is to say, "God, please help me see the possibilities you can create, even when it feels as though I'm surrounded by impossibilities."

What about you? What dream have you stopped praying for? And is there any reason why today can't be the day you run to Jesus in desperation?

3. GOD, GIVE ME FAITH TO SAY, "EVEN IF YOU DON'T"

In Daniel 3, you'll find a story about three Jewish men named Shadrach, Meshach, and Abednego. You may be familiar with the story as a whole, but there's a specific detail I want to point out that can help us reestablish our connection with God through prayer.

The king of Babylon, Nebuchadnezzar, commissioned a golden statue to be built—and not just any statue, but an incredible construction that was ninety feet tall and nine feet wide. When it was finished, the king assembled all the people within his province around the statue and commanded that they bow before it in worship. According to Nebuchadnezzar, anyone who refused to worship the idol would be thrown into a blazing furnace to be killed.

Of course, this entire production created a difficult decision for the three Jewish men. Do they bow down to a golden statue, an idol, or do they honor God and get thrown into a fiery oven? They chose to honor God, and this is what happened next:

> Nebuchadnezzar said to them, "Is it true, Shadrach, Meshach, and Abednego, that you refuse to serve my gods or to worship the gold statue I have set up? I will give you one more chance to bow down and worship the statue I have made when you hear the sound of the musical instruments. But if you refuse, you will be thrown immediately into the blazing furnace. And then what god will be able to rescue you from my power?"
>
> Shadrach, Meshach, and Abednego replied, "O Nebuchadnezzar, we do not need to defend ourselves before you. If we are thrown into the blazing furnace, the God whom we serve is able to save us. He will rescue us from your power, Your Majesty. But *even if he doesn't*, we want to make it clear to you, Your Majesty, that we will never serve your gods or worship the gold statue you have set up." (Dan. 3:14–18, emphasis mine)

Mic drop! Obviously, that's a powerful moment of faith even in the most dangerous of circumstances. But there's one important detail that stands out to me. One particular phrase: "even if he doesn't . . ."

Why was that important? Because Shadrach, Meshach, and Abednego were not going to allow their circumstances to define their obedience to God; nor would they allow circumstances to define their understanding of God's character. This was a real furnace, with real fire, and they were facing real death. Their futures and their dreams were about to go up in smoke—literally! But they had the faith in the face of that adversity to declare that they would not bow down and worship a false god. They were confident in God's character and chose to worship Him for who He is over what He does.

"Even if he doesn't" meant they understood God could choose to save them from the fire, or He might not. But either way, He was still their God!

Being a man of his word, King Nebuchadnezzar threw Shadrach, Meshach, and Abednego into the fire, expecting them to die. But remember what we said earlier? Anything is possible with God!

> But suddenly, Nebuchadnezzar jumped up in amazement and exclaimed to his advisers, "Didn't we tie up three men and throw them into the furnace?"
>
> "Yes, Your Majesty, we certainly did," they replied.
>
> "Look!" Nebuchadnezzar shouted. "I see four men, unbound, walking around in the fire unharmed! And the fourth looks like a god!"
>
> Then Nebuchadnezzar came as close as he could to the door of the flaming furnace and shouted: "Shadrach, Meshach, and Abednego, servants of the Most High God, come out! Come here!"
>
> So Shadrach, Meshach, and Abednego stepped out of the fire. Then the high officers, officials, governors, and advisers crowded around them and saw that the fire had not touched them. Not a hair on their heads was singed, and their clothing was not scorched. They didn't even smell of smoke! (Dan. 3:24–27)

Yes! God was in the furnace with the three men. They didn't die in the fire. Their hair didn't get singed, and they didn't even smell like smoke! In other words, they were in the fire, but not a part of the fire.

I don't know what type of circumstances you're facing or what furnace you're in, but I do know God is standing beside you. He is in the fire with you. You may feel the intensity of the heat, you may be scared, and you may think you're all alone. Or it may feel as if your dreams are on fire, and you may feel discouraged and uncertain of the future.

Either way, God is in the furnace with you, and He will protect you. Let the words of Jesus comfort your heart: "And be sure of this: I am with you always, even to the end of the age" (Matt. 28:20). Jesus never said we wouldn't spend time in a furnace, but He did promise that He would be with us wherever we go—even if it means standing by our side amidst the flames.

GOD IS STANDING BESIDE YOU. HE IS IN THE FIRE WITH YOU.

Because that's true, you can make "even if You don't" an important part of your prayer life—especially as you learn to dream again and rekindle your intimacy with God. "Lord, I feel like You are opening doors for a dream I thought had died a long time ago. But even if You don't, I still trust You. I still proclaim that You are good and faithful and gracious. And I still worship You, Lord God."

We're all going to experience pain and loss, and we're all going to go through times when it feels as though our dreams are dying. As my friend Katherine discovered, it's not easy to keep praying when it feels as if our words have hit a concrete ceiling on their way to heaven and bounced back down. It's much easier to switch to safe prayers that risk little or nothing so we don't risk feeling rejected again.

I get it. I know it's not easy, and I'm not about to pretend there's a simple fix. But I do want to encourage you to remember that bold prayers honor God, and God honors bold prayers.

When you feel like your prayers are hitting a lid, tell God about it. Remember, communication unlocks intimacy. If you don't know where to start the conversation or how to pray, that's okay too. Start right there. Ask God to help you see His character over your circumstances, to find possibilities when impossibilities surround you, and to give you the faith to declare that "even if He doesn't," you will still worship Him.

As we end this chapter, I'd like to challenge you to take a moment right now to communicate with God. To pray. Maybe you've never prayed before, and that's okay. Just start by talking with God as if He were sitting next to you. Tell Him your hopes and dreams, and ask for His strength to help you chase those dreams and see them come true.

Maybe you used to pray boldly and approach God filled with faith, but like my friend Katherine, you've been wounded and you feel defeated. Perhaps you've been beaten down by years of things not going how you hoped they'd go—by prayers not answered in the way you wanted them to be. If that's you, make a decision right now to restore that connection. Ask God to help you trust His character over your circumstances. Ask Him to help you find possibilities when you're surrounded by the impossible. And declare with faith and trust that you will follow God and retain your connection with Him *even if* He doesn't respond the way you hope.

I'm confident that these three prayers will deepen your intimacy with God and help you restore your connection with Him. Just as importantly, I'm confident that rebuilding your prayer life will provide an incredible boost as you continue along this path of chasing your God-sized dreams.

BOLD PRAYERS HONOR GOD, AND GOD HONORS BOLD PRAYERS.

eight

WHAT'S SO SCARY ABOUT THE HOLY SPIRIT?

The Spirit is the first power we practically experience,
but the last power we come to understand.

—OSWALD CHAMBERS[1]

It happened all the time when I was growing up.

I'd be walking through the house, minding my own business and totally unaware that anything was about to happen, when my dad would jump out from behind a door or under a bed or inside some other unexpected place and yell "*Boo!*" at the top of his lungs. Then, after I finished flailing my arms and crying out in terror, Dad would take me by the shoulders and ask, "Hey, Josh, what's so scary about the word *boo*?"

Still trying to catch my breath, I would answer with something like "Nothing, Dad. What's scary is you jumping out of a laundry basket and grabbing my leg." Then we'd laugh together, and I'd try to keep up my guard for the next time I'd hear that dreaded word *boo*.

You know the saying, "The apple doesn't fall far from the tree"? Well, I was walking through Walmart when I noticed an aisle with dozens of Halloween masks on clearance. And I had an idea.

About thirty minutes later, there was a Walmart bag in the trash and a scary gorilla mask on my head, and I was hiding in the tub in our boys' bathroom. I shook with glee when I heard my wife call out from downstairs, "Okay, Nehemiah, time to go upstairs and take your shower." *Game time!*

I heard the sound of my son's feet thumping up the stairs. Then I saw his hand reach behind the shower curtain toward the faucet. And that's when I realized I hadn't fully thought through my plan. I was hiding in a bathtub, fully clothed, wearing a gorilla mask—and about to take a shower.

Panicking a little, I reached up and grabbed Nehemiah's hand before he could turn on the water. Confused and probably a little curious, he peeked his head behind the curtain—and locked eyes with me. Or, rather, I locked eyes with my son, but he locked eyes with a terrifying gorilla crouched unexpectedly in his bathtub.

After screaming for what felt like a full twenty seconds, Nehemiah ran out of the bathroom at a dead sprint. Feeling guilty, I jumped up and ran after him to try to provide some comfort—but I forgot that I was still wearing the gorilla mask. I ended up chasing my son around the house until I finally remembered to take off the mask and reveal myself as his tormentor.

Later that night, Nehemiah and I were laughing together about the whole incident when I asked, "Hey, Neo, what's so scary about a gorilla anyway?"

He looked at me with complete sincerity and said, "Nothing—when I see them at the zoo."

In a similar way, most of us aren't scared of the Holy Spirit when we hear about Him during a sermon on Sunday morning. But when it comes to figuring out how we should interact with the Spirit on a daily basis, and especially when it comes to things like spiritual gifts and other expressions of the Holy Spirit's ministry in our lives—that's a different story.

Then things can get really scary really quickly. In fact, because the Holy Spirit has been misunderstood and misused by people in the church for centuries, we've gotten to a place where many followers of Jesus are terrified of the very Spirit God intended to be their greatest earthly companion.

Obviously, that's a problem for following Jesus. It's also a problem for those of us with a passion to pursue God-sized dreams, because the Holy Spirit is our primary Advocate—our most active Helper—when it comes to not only chasing those dreams but also living life with hope.

In the previous chapter, we explored the importance of gaining intimacy with God through prayer. Now we are going to learn more about the gift of the Holy Spirit, who helps us pursue our God-sized dreams. Let's take some time to gain a broader understanding of who the Holy Spirit is, how He guides us in the pursuit of our dreams, and how we can align ourselves with His voice in order to experience His power.

UNDERSTANDING THE HOLY SPIRIT

The first thing we need to understand about the Holy Spirit is that He is God. He's not a "force." He's not a manifestation of the universe. The Holy Spirit is God Himself.

It's also a common misconception for people to think the Holy Spirit is *part* of God—specifically, a third of God. It's true that God exists as a Trinity. He is one Being made up of three Persons—the Father, the Son, and the Holy Spirit—which is pretty much impossible for us to understand because it's so far outside of our experience. But it's important for us to know that God is one, not divided into three. When the Father spoke to Moses on Mount Sinai and gave him the Ten Commandments, that was God speaking. When Jesus taught His disciples in Galilee, that was God speaking. And when the Holy Spirit speaks to our hearts, sparks new dreams, and supports us as we chase those dreams—that is God speaking too.

Thankfully, you don't have to rely on my opinion about the Holy Spirit. You can learn about Him directly from the words of Jesus:

> I will ask the Father, and he will give you another Advocate, who will never leave you. He is the Holy Spirit, who leads into all truth. The world cannot receive him, because it isn't looking for him and doesn't recognize him. But you know him, because he lives with you now and later will be in you. No, I will not abandon you as orphans—I will come to you. Soon the world will no longer see me, but you will see me. Since I live, you also will live. (John 14:16–19)

Jesus described the Holy Spirit as our "Advocate." That word means someone who provides comfort, strengthens what is weak, and counsels those who need wisdom. The Holy Spirit is the person who will comfort us when we are hurt by the happenings of life, give us strength when we feel too weak to continue, and counsel us when we are unclear of what direction to go. What an important gift from God that we can't leave unopened and unused!

But there's more. Jesus said this Advocate "lives with you now" and "will never leave you." When we become followers of God, we receive God Himself into our hearts and minds—He joins us in a way we'll never understand through scientific examination. The Spirit guides us to a deeper understanding of truth, and He will never leave us.

So let me ask: What's so scary about the Holy Spirit? Why would we ever distance ourselves from such an incredible gift?

Those are good questions, and I think there are two main answers. First, throughout Christian history and continuing today, leaders in the church along with everyday Christians have made claims about the Holy Spirit and acted in ways that go beyond what Scripture teaches. These claims range from genuinely misunderstanding the Spirit's role to outright abuse and falsehood.

For example, I remember standing in line as a child at church and then repeating certain phrases over and over again. The goal was to see if I was one of the chosen "holy people" who were able to speak in tongues. Now, I believe the gifts of the Holy Spirit mentioned in Scripture are real and that they remain active in the church today. But the way my church handled things by singling out specific individuals as extra holy was not biblical, and I know it caused both confusion and pain for me as a young person.

In my experience, we often focus on the spiritual gifts when it comes to the Holy Spirit's work in our lives—which means we often miss out on His overall purpose. As we've read, the Holy Spirit was sent to be our Advocate in all areas. Too often we make spiritual gifts a measuring tool of holiness, which often causes wounds. It's a way for us to say, "I'm more spiritual than you." But the Holy Spirit's role is not for you to look holy on Sunday morning; it's to counsel and equip you to live a life of purpose and hope every day of the week.

Then there is the other end of the spectrum, where people are encouraged to bark like dogs or pick up poisonous snakes, all in the name of the Holy Spirit. Or, worst of all, those TV programs where "pastors" claim the Holy Spirit will heal you of any disease as soon as you send that donation check to their ministries. After seeing the Spirit abused in these ways, it's no wonder people start to fear or disregard God's gift to us.

Similarly, many regular Christians abuse the Holy Spirit by claiming the Spirit directed them to believe ideas or act in ways that are contrary to God's Word. For example, you have probably seen news footage of people from a specific "church" holding up hate-filled signs and protesting outside of funerals—or at parades—claiming to be guided by God's Spirit. You may know people who have used the Spirit to justify actions or attitudes that are otherwise harmful. I've even had people tell me, "I feel the Spirit telling me to have an affair."

Let me make it clear: if you feel led to do something or believe something that clearly goes against the teaching of the Bible, you are *not* being led by the Holy Spirit. And the same is true for anyone close to you who makes such a claim. The Holy Spirit never contradicts the character of God or His Word.

On a personal level, I remember when my brother Matthew, who is a wonderful man, worked up the courage to tell our family that he was gay. He was a teenager at the time, and his announcement was a bit of a shock for our conservative family. (This was twenty years ago, when Christians were still sweeping the issue of homosexuality under the rug.) My parents went to their church leaders for wisdom and advice, but basically the only thing they were told was that Matthew could no longer sing with the worship team. In fact, they were told that if Matthew *did* sing on Sunday morning, he would quench the presence of the Holy Spirit. At a time when my sixteen-year-old brother needed his church family the most, he was instead rejected and ostracized—all in the name of the Holy Spirit.

That's destructive. And abusive. And it causes regular Christians like you and me to feel afraid of the Holy Spirit when we should be seeking Him each day.

The second reason many Christians are confused about the Holy Spirit is that many churches and denominations basically ignore Him. Many church leaders want to avoid the excesses and abuses of the Holy Spirit I just described, but in doing so, they go the other direction and focus their teaching and attention on God the Father and Jesus the Son, failing to instruct their congregations about how the Spirit—our Advocate—speaks to us, guides us, and empowers us to chase our dreams.

The way this plays out practically is that we are told, whether directly or indirectly, that our connection with God is a one-way street. We are instructed to read the Bible and apply it to our lives, and we are encouraged to pray and express to God what's on our hearts and minds—but everything stays with us. We are not taught that the Holy Spirit *answers* our prayers by leading us, guiding us, and offering what we need. We're not taught that the Spirit helps us understand and apply the Scriptures by leading us into all truth.

This is also harmful. And it has a big impact on our ability to pursue our dreams, because it means we try to chase a God-sized dream without the incredible gift of God Himself leading us, speaking to us, and strengthening us from within.

> THE SPIRIT IS THE VERY SOURCE THAT HELPS US FIND DIRECTION, GIVES US STRENGTH, AND BRINGS HOPE TO OUR JOURNEY.

Let me be clear: we cannot abuse or abandon the Holy Spirit and expect to stay on course as we pursue our God-sized dreams and our hopes for the future. That's because the Spirit is the very Source that helps us find direction, gives us strength, and brings hope to our journey every step of the way.

DISCERNING GOD'S WILL

"Pastor Josh, how do I know God's will for my life?" "Pastor, how can I hear God's voice?" "How will I know if this is the right decision for me and my family?"

I get asked those questions a lot. I mean, *a whole lot.* And I understand why. For most Christians, including myself, learning how to hear from God and discern His will for our lives is a critical issue. Because if we believe God is real and He cares about us, then certainly He wants to guide us in some way. But if it's up to us to figure out which direction God is leading, how can we ever be sure we're interpreting His instructions correctly?

This is especially true as we seek to pursue our God-sized dreams. How can we know if those dreams are from God and honor God, or if they are totally separate from His plan and purpose for our lives?

Thankfully, there's one simple answer to those questions: the Holy Spirit. That's how we hear and heed God's will, and that's how we walk forward in confidence toward our dreams and into our futures.

Listen again to the gospel of John, where Jesus taught His disciples about the Holy Spirit:

> But now I am going away to the one who sent me, and not one of you is asking where I am going. Instead, you grieve because of what I've told you. But in fact, it is best for you that I go away, because if I don't, the Advocate won't come. If I do go away, then I will send him to you. (16:5–7)

Lots of people think of the Holy Spirit as a heavenly Plan B. We know Jesus came to teach us about God and to lay down His life as our Savior. But it's as though we think God had to figure out another way to interact with us once Jesus rose again and ascended to heaven. "I know," we imagine Him saying, "I'll send a less important person to earth to talk with my children there, and I'll call Him the Holy Spirit."

That's not the way it worked. Look at what Jesus said: "it is best" that He return to heaven so that those of us on earth could receive the Holy Spirit. Our Advocate. Our Helper. Jesus didn't say, "Everything will work itself out." He didn't say, "The Advocate will be good enough until I get back." He said sending the Holy Spirit was "best."

In other words, the Holy Spirit was, is, and always will be Plan A when it comes to God leading and directing His people in finding His will for their lives.

You might be thinking, *Okay, great, the Holy Spirit helps us find God's will—but how does that work? How do we determine what is God's will and what is not? How do we discern which way the Holy Spirit is moving and where He wants us to go?*

To answer that, we need to understand there are two layers involved with what we typically refer to as "God's will for my life." Those are God's universal will for the lives of His people, and God's personal will for our individual lives.

God's Universal Will

When I ask *What is God's will for my life?* the first answer is that Jesus wants me to live as His disciple—as a member of His kingdom who thinks the way He thought and acts the way He acted. There are many things that all Christians should believe and do as part of God's universal will for our lives.

Of course, we don't have space to unpack every aspect of God's universal will, but here's a great example from the words of Jesus. It's what we often refer to as the Great Commandment:

> Jesus replied, "'You must love the LORD your God with all your heart, all your soul, and all your mind.' This is the first and greatest commandment. A second is equally important: 'Love your neighbor as yourself.' The entire law

and all the demands of the prophets are based on these two commandments." (Matt. 22:37–40)

These commandments are expressions of God's will. I can say with certainty that it's God's will for my life that I love Him with all my heart, soul, and mind. You can say with certainty that it's God's will for your life to love your neighbor as yourself. Meaning, if you are contemplating something that will harm your neighbor, you can be sure that it's not part of God's will for you.

Here's another example from the gospel of Matthew:

Jesus came and told his disciples, "I have been given all authority in heaven and on earth. Therefore, go and make disciples of all the nations, baptizing them in the name of the Father and the Son and the Holy Spirit. Teach these new disciples to obey all the commands I have given you. And be sure of this: I am with you always, even to the end of the age." (28:18–20)

We often refer to these verses as the Great Commission, and they are also part of God's universal will. It's God's will for you to help make disciples of Jesus—to teach those among your friends and family about God and the gospel, to help them obey what they learn, and to lead them toward baptism as fully mature members of God's kingdom.

The rest of God's Word also defines and supports God's universal will. The psalms show us that worship is part of God's plan for our lives. The proverbs show us that God values wisdom. And the Ten Commandments are more than just good rules to follow; they're guidelines that help define God's will for us.

All of these represent God's will for our lives, and we can feel confident when we are operating within the boundaries, instructions, and guidelines God has given us through Scripture.

God's Personal Will

I can almost hear you thinking, *But what about* me? *What about God's will for my life, specifically?* I agree that's where it gets confusing. It's a lot easier for me to understand God's universal will than to find His will for me personally.

I know God has a specific plan for my life as Joshua Gagnon—husband, father, pastor, and international man of mystery. (I'm still waiting on that last part.) God has a specific will for what He wants to accomplish in me and through me. The same is true for you. God has a plan for your life. So how do you discover it?

Imagine a family dinner at which the father brings out a big script and begins shouting commands at his children. He tells each one when to take a bite, when to ask a question, when to wipe their face with a napkin, and so on. How long would it take you to decide that you were observing a dysfunctional family—a dysfunctional father?

Yet that's often how we expect God to show us His will for our lives. We want Him to have a divine instruction manual with our names on it, and we want Him to read out the next step we're supposed to take whenever we pray for wisdom or ask for direction. We want Him to tell us exactly what to do and when to do it.

Instead of a father with a script, imagine a father sitting down with his children and rolling out a huge piece of paper across the table. Then he gets out a shiny new box of crayons and says, "Let's create something together!" This version is a better picture of God's plan and purpose for our lives.

It's been said that God's will is more like a match than a map. I love that! Rather than giving us turn-by-turn directions on where are lives are supposed to go, God uses our dreams and desires to create a spark in our hearts. He's interested not in ordering us around like soldiers but rather in lighting a fire in our lives and watching us bring light and love to a darkened world.

That's why our hopes and our God-sized dreams are so critical. They are expressions of God's will for our lives! You don't have to ask, "God, am I supposed to follow this dream?" Instead, the fact that you have a dream burning in your heart is evidence that God is working—that He is actively communicating His will to you. As a result, our dreams grow and change. And as we pursue our dreams through the different seasons of our lives, we grow and change. We may even let go of certain dreams and chase new ones—not because the old dreams weren't worthwhile, but because we've grown into something new.

This is why the Holy Spirit is such an important part of our lives. As we begin to pursue our dreams, the Spirit will either fan the flame of that dream or snuff it out and send us in a new direction. We need to be listening, and we need to be willing to follow where He leads.

That's where discernment comes into play. Not everything that knocks on the door of our hearts is good for us. As we go about our daily lives, and especially as we make important decisions, we have opportunities to discern where the Holy Spirit is guiding us.

NOT EVERYTHING THAT KNOCKS ON THE DOOR OF OUR HEARTS IS GOOD FOR US.

Here's the heart of the matter: there is a generation of Christians today who believe that God's will is black or white, right or wrong. They believe there are only two paths, and only one is God's will; the other is definitely not. This belief creates fear, and it doesn't allow for the kind of freedom God desires for our lives. It keeps us from moving forward with boldness and joy.

Instead, we need to remember God's character. He is good. He loves us and wants the best for us. Therefore, we can confidently pursue our dreams with the knowledge that He will lead us in the right direction when we are aligned with His Spirit.

FOLLOWING THE SPIRIT'S LEAD

I grew up on a small lake in New Hampshire, where I loved to go fishing. I must have caught hundreds of bass during my years on that lake, although I'm sure they were nowhere near as large as I remember. I didn't have a motorboat, so I paddled my way around the lake in a canoe.

One day while I was fighting my way through the choppy waters and wishing I had a boat with an engine, a local rowing team passed me by. I floated past them in awe—they were poetry in motion. I'd seen professional rowing while watching the Olympics, but seeing this team in person was so impressive!

Rowing teams use a boat known as a racing shell, which is tiny since the goal of the sport is to reach your maximum speed. There are eight people in the shell, each pulling their oars over thirty times a minute. If one person's rhythm is off, the racing shell will lose speed and may tip over. If unison is broken for even a moment, the boat won't go straight. If one person's oar goes deeper into the water than another's, the boat will rock and slow down. And if one person stands up and decides to dance, they will tip the racing shell and get kicked off the team. (Don't ask me how I know that.)

For rowers, getting up to top speed takes perfect coordination, perfect timing, and perfect positioning. Even the smallest detail out of alignment will stop the team from achieving its full potential.

In the same way that a rowing team needs to work in unison, you and I need to live in alignment with the Holy Spirit. The apostle Paul declared in Galatians 5:24–25: "Those who belong to Christ Jesus have nailed the passions and desires of their sinful nature to his cross and crucified them there. Since we are living by the Spirit, let us follow the Spirit's leading in every part of our lives."

We are at our best when we are aligned with the Holy Spirit—when we are aware of His leading and when we allow Him to open doors or close them as He sees fit. As we close out this chapter, let's look at three practical steps we can take to gain that kind of alignment with the Spirit. Because remember:

alignment with the Holy Spirit is essential to chasing and realizing our God-given dreams.

1. Acknowledge Your Need for God's Spirit

I love it when Jennifer or my boys acknowledge their need for me. When Jennifer approaches me and says something like "Hey, strong man, can you open this jar for me?" it makes me feel so needed. Though there have been times when my eyes almost popped out of my head trying to open those jars, I can't let her down when she needs me.

Similarly, it's important for us to acknowledge our need for the Holy Spirit's guidance and direction in our lives. We need to recognize the critical role the Spirit plays in our lives and in the fulfillment of our dreams.

This isn't for His benefit, of course, but for ours. The Spirit is well aware of our frailness and our uncertainty. It benefits us when we acknowledge our need for God's Spirit. We have far too much history with trying (and failing) to live and dream and find fulfillment in our own strength. We don't do ourselves any good by pretending to have it all together.

I like the way David acknowledged his need for God in Psalm 63:1: "O God, you are my God; I earnestly search for you. My soul thirsts for you; my whole body longs for you in this parched and weary land where there is no water."

Acknowledging our need for the Spirit is especially helpful when the going gets tough. When you hit a rough patch and you feel a desire to quit—especially a desire to quit pursuing your God-sized dreams—take a step back. Cry out to God and acknowledge your weakness, your inability to figure things out. Proclaim your trust in His goodness and His guidance, and ask the Holy Spirit to give you what you need to keep going.

2. Be Aware of the Spirit's Voice

Jennifer and I grew up in completely different environments. My mom did my laundry and cooked dinners each night for the family in a "traditional" mothering role. Jennifer's home was more independent. If you wanted your clothes clean, you washed them; when you were hungry, you made yourself something to eat.

Early in our marriage, I expected Jen to be like my mom—to take care of me, basically. I remember feeling so frustrated because all of my expectations weren't being met. I used to pray that God would help her see I was right and that she needed to change. (I know, I know—husband of the year!)

I can still remember the road I was driving down when God finally responded to my prayer. I was again asking God to change her ways when I heard the Holy Spirit whisper to my heart, *You can pray for her to become your perfect wife, or you can pray that she grows into the woman I desire for her to be.*

I was floored. Speechless for a moment. Every hair on the back of my neck stood on end. Then I said out loud, "God, I want her to become everything You desire for her!"

From that day on, I have supported who Jen is becoming in Christ instead of who I want her to be. I've watched her become an amazing woman who follows after Jesus with her whole heart, and I couldn't ask for a better wife.

There are people who hear that story and ask, "Do you really think that was God speaking to you?"

Yes, I do. When we align ourselves with the Holy Spirit, we

will hear His voice. This probably won't be an audible thing—I've never heard the Holy Spirit speak to me audibly, though people I respect claim to have heard Him—but it doesn't have to be audible for it to be meaningful. And powerful.

The simplest, most common way we can hear the Holy Spirit's voice is through the Bible. Really, the Bible *is* God's voice, just written down for us to study and enjoy. And I believe there will be moments in your life when the Holy Spirit uses specific passages of His Word to speak to you, loudly and directly.

I personally experience this as a shock of understanding when the Spirit calls out a specific verse or passage. I'll be reading, and then it's like a lightning bolt goes off in my brain. I know in that moment, without a doubt, that *these words are for me.* In that moment, God's Spirit is guiding me and directing me through His Word. You may experience that guidance differently, but if you are faithful in studying the Scriptures, you *will* hear the Spirit's voice. Your job is to be aware of what He wants to say, and then to obey.

> YOUR JOB IS TO BE AWARE OF WHAT HE WANTS TO SAY, AND THEN TO OBEY.

The Holy Spirit also speaks to us in what I think of as whispers. These are thoughts that come into our minds but do not originate in our minds. They are gentle nudges that encourage us to keep moving in a specific direction—or that we are going the wrong way and need to turn back. "Say you're sorry." "Pray with that person." "Remember that your sins have been forgiven; you don't need to carry them." These are the kinds of whispers I hear from the Holy Spirit, and I cherish them. I have trained myself to listen for them, and you can as well.

Similarly, the Holy Spirit often speaks to us through the people we interact with in our daily lives. God loves to use His children to communicate His heart to us. Sometimes this is a direct, almost supernatural experience. I've had people call me and say, "I feel like God is moving me to tell you something." Most of the time it's more subtle. People will share something that hits me right in the heart, or a child will say something that speaks directly to a situation I'm facing, and I'll know the Holy Spirit is behind it.

This isn't an exhaustive list. We can hear the Spirit's voice through nature, through our circumstances, through music, and through a host of other sources. The point is that we need to be aware that the Holy Spirit is real, and we need to maintain an awareness that His voice can guide us at any moment—as long as we're listening.

We need to be especially aware of and yearning for the Holy Spirit's voice as we pursue our God-sized dreams. Here's the great news: He will speak! He's not silent. He planted those dreams inside us, and He will whisper, shout, speak through others, speak through His Word, and more as we chase the tomorrow He's planned for us to find.

3. Maintain Alignment

Just as with the rowing team I mentioned earlier, it takes effort to maintain alignment between ourselves and the Holy Spirit. Once we get into that rhythm where we hear His voice and understand how He is guiding us to pursue our dreams, we must not become complacent. We need to keep up the pace and work to maintain unity.

One factor that will knock us out of alignment with God's

Spirit faster than just about anything else is drifting into patterns of sin. Yes, we all make mistakes, and we will continue to make mistakes this side of eternity. Thank God for the forgiveness we have received in Jesus Christ! But there's something different at play when we allow ourselves to make a habit or a routine of sinful choices. Even in a culture that is offended by the idea of sin, it still remains true that God desires for us to be holy and trust in His grace when we're tempted to step outside of alignment and into sin.

The author of Hebrews wrote, "Therefore, since we are surrounded by such a huge crowd of witnesses to the life of faith, let us strip off every weight that slows us down, especially the sin that so easily trips us up. And let us run with endurance the race God has set before us" (12:1). You've seen how choices can "trip us up"—choices such as greed, gossip, lying, pornography, laziness, pride, and so on. In order to maintain alignment with the Holy Spirit, get rid of such things as soon as you become aware of their presence in your life.

The other way we can disrupt our alignment with the Holy Spirit is when we start to believe we have everything figured out. We start to neglect the disciplines that keep us connected to the Spirit—reading the Bible, prayer, worship, generosity, fellowship with other Christians, and so on. The more we try to take back control of our lives, the more we are in danger of losing our unity with God's Spirit and ignoring His guidance.

Every relationship is two-sided by definition, and our relationship with the Holy Spirit is no exception. It's our responsibility to steward our side of the relationship by acknowledging our need for His presence, staying aware of His voice, and maintaining our alignment in every way possible.

The Holy Spirit isn't a scary gorilla hiding behind your shower curtain. I understand the baggage that often gets in the way of us understanding His purpose in our lives, and I know He's been abused, misused, and often ignored. But let me be very clear about this truth: the Holy Spirit is an amazing gift from God, and He is given to each of us as our Advocate. He's our teammate here on earth who helps guide our dreams and provides hope and strength when we feel discouraged or lost. He is with us now, and He will never leave us. Never! He is waiting for you *in this very moment* to listen to His whispers, call out for His help, and depend on His direction.

THE HOLY SPIRIT IS THE
PERSON WHO WILL COMFORT
US WHEN WE ARE HURT BY
THE HAPPENINGS OF LIFE,
GIVE US STRENGTH WHEN
WE FEEL TOO WEAK TO
CONTINUE, AND COUNSEL US
WHEN WE ARE UNCLEAR OF
WHAT DIRECTION TO GO.

nine

FINISH STRONG

Beginning well is a momentary thing; finishing well is a
lifelong thing.

—RAVI ZACHARIAS[1]

There's a brief season in New England that people in the rest
of the country call "spring." We call it "home-project season."
This is the time of year when the snow finally starts to melt
and people emerge from their houses to bask in the warm sun
for what seems like the first time in months.

Then, when the basking is finished, it's time to get to
work. Time to rake up all the leaves still damp and matted
down from snow. Time to pick up all the branches that were
tumbled from trees by the winds of nor'easters. Time to paint
the decks and attempt to wash the salt off our cars.

I love spring! It's a new season, a fresh start, and a time
for new dreams.

On one particular spring day, Jennifer and I were putting together our to-do lists for outside projects. We'd moved into a new home the previous fall, and this was our first real chance to make changes to the exterior. My job was to paint the upstairs balcony, which was in pretty bad shape. Jen's job was to repaint the shutters from green to black after I removed them from all the windows around the house.

I'd rented a hydraulic lift from Home Depot, and I was working on the balcony when Jen came outside. "See you soon, honey," she said. "I'm picking up the boys from school."

By that time, I was ready for a break from balcony painting. Or, more accurately, I was ready for a break from standing precariously way up high in a hydraulic lift, risking my life to paint a balcony. So as Jen's car pulled out into the road, I lowered myself back down to the ground where I belonged.

That's when I had an idea. I decided to surprise my wife by giving her a head start on her project. I calculated how long it would take her to get to school and back, and I decided I would have just enough time to take down one of the sixteen shutters, paint it, and get it rehung before she got home. *This time I'll show you how it's done, Chip Gaines!*

Everything went exactly as I planned. I took down one of the shutters from the front of the house, got it painted, and then put it back looking all shiny and new. When Jen and the boys pulled in the driveway, I was sitting casually on the porch. I worked on my poker face so I wouldn't give away the surprise.

As soon as she got out of the car, Jen asked, "Why did you bring the lift out front?"

I answered with a wry smile. "No reason." I resisted the

urge to look over at the shutter, because I wanted her to see it for herself and think, *That's my man!*

Unfortunately, Jen wasn't buying it. "Joshua," she said, "what did you do?" Did I mention I have a terrible poker face?

I was ready for my reward, so I gestured toward the window with my chin and said, "Shutter."

Jennifer freaked out, jumping up and down and clapping her hands together. "I love it!" she cried. "Thank you so much! And let me know when you finish the next one." Then she gave me a big hug and shuffled our boys up the stairs and inside.

Filled with pride, I stood on the lawn and admired my work for a full thirty seconds before Jennifer's words really landed. "Let me know when you finish the next one . . ." *Oh no. Wait a minute! What have I started?* And then it hit me: I had painted one shutter on the front of the house. In my excitement and rush to get things done quickly, I'd failed to realize the placement would leave one black shutter in a sea of fifteen green shutters. Leaving them like that would be an eyesore.

There's no way out, I thought. *Now I have to remove, paint, and rehang fifteen more shutters!* Sure enough, for the rest of that day and most of the next, I begrudgingly finished what I'd started.

I've learned that, in most cases, starting something is much more exciting than finishing it. Getting started requires little more than a dream or a passion, while finishing requires lots and lots of work, faith, and resiliency. Once we start something, we often develop the fear of failure and the ever-present concern that when we finally achieve what we've been dreaming about for so long, it won't be the amazing experience we've been expecting.

As we move into the final pages of this book, I want to

challenge you not only to begin pursuing your dreams but to catch them. Can you imagine what it would be like to live out your dream and to chase after your desired future with the same urgency, commitment, faith, and passion you had when you first began?

It can happen! I've seen it happen many times in my life and in the lives of others. But it won't happen by accident. You'll need to decide daily that you will finish strong.

RUN TO WIN

If you spent a week in our home, you would hear me say "Finish strong" lots of times. It's one of my go-to expressions as a father because I believe it's a critical principle for life.

Specifically, I've taught my sons that finishing strong is not the act of completing something but the process we go through on our way to completion. The moment we start something, the process of finishing begins; therefore, how we choose to live in the gap between the starting line and finish line will determine how we actually end the journey.

I like how the apostle Paul phrased this idea: "Don't you realize that in a race everyone runs, but only one person gets the prize? So run to win!" (1 Cor. 9:24).

In a race, nobody stands at the end trying to talk the runners out of achieving their dreams, and no runner willingly quits before crossing the finish line. Instead, the fight to finish well takes place during the race itself. It's during the difficult parts that we are tempted to quit. That's why we aren't really celebrating the completion of a race when a runner breaks through the tape; we're celebrating all the miles that were conquered on the way to reaching the end.

However, we as a culture are much better at starting things than we are at finishing them. For example, it seems as if everyone in America loves weddings—we even watch TV shows of other people's dream weddings just to entertain ourselves. But those shows fail to teach us how to finish strong within a lifetime commitment.

There are many more examples of this: We love signing up for gym memberships, but we rarely hit our weight-loss goals. We love opening new credit cards, but we're not disciplined in making payments. We're great at starting families, but we find it much more difficult to keep them intact. We show up on the first day of work with a lot of passion and promise, but then we find ourselves going through the motions months later.

Unfortunately, we're also not great at finishing strong when it comes to following Jesus. New Christians are usually taught the importance of reading their Bibles, praying, serving, finding a community, and more. But when life happens, and they feel the resistance that inevitably comes from our spiritual Enemy, many lose their enthusiasm. This isn't a new phenomenon either. Look at what God said to the church at Ephesus in Revelation 2:4: "But I have this complaint against you. You don't love me or each other as you did at first!"

In our time together, I hope you've been encouraged to believe it's not over for you. I hope God has given you new dreams, shown you past dreams that are ready to be replaced, and reenergized those that were dormant. And I hope your prayer life shakes heaven with a newfound boldness.

Yet, as much as I believe God can and will do these things,

I'm not naive to the reality that the excitement you may feel now won't last forever. You will face opposition; the winds will blow, and the waves will seem overpowering. There will be times when you feel like a grounded eagle, injured by life and tempted to forget you were created to soar. In those moments, it often seems easier to quit than believe God will help us reach our dreams. I speak from experience.

Because of this, I want to equip you with some tools that will help you press on and finish strong. Specifically, let's explore the benefits of managing your expectations, fighting back against discouragement, and focusing on what you can control.

MANAGE YOUR EXPECTATIONS

At the beginning of the chapter, I told you about painting our upstairs balcony. Well, it was not very fun. Fun was actually nowhere to be found. And I remember vividly being perched at the top of a forty-foot hydraulic lift and thinking, *The best thing for us to do is just sell this house, because I don't want to ever do this again.*

That's a pretty good example of failing to finish strong. And one of the main reasons I got so frustrated up there (other than my knees knocking so loudly you could physically hear them, and my life being in jeopardy) was because I went into that particular project with unrealistic expectations. *Paint the balcony?* I thought. *No problem. I'll just rent a lift and be done in a couple of hours.*

The same is true with our dreams. In fact, I'm convinced

the only way to finish strong in the pursuit of our dreams is to start and run each race with realistic expectations.

Jesus talked about that very thing in one of his most famous teachings: "But don't begin until you count the cost. For who would begin construction of a building without first calculating the cost to see if there is enough money to finish it?" (Luke 14:28).

It's easy to read those two sentences and think, *Duh. What kind of idiot would begin construction without a good estimate of the project's cost?* But it happens all the time. And not just exterior painting projects. (I'm raising my hand here.)

I regularly ask people in premarital counseling one of the most important questions any couple can think through: "How will you resolve your first fight?" Usually their answer is "Oh, we won't fight. We never fight! We get along perfectly."

I've had that conversation dozens of times, and each time I still feel shocked by the naivety of their response. My first instinct is to blurt out, "What?! You think you'll never fight? That's ridiculous. I hope you get in a fight on the way home from this appointment just so you'll get knocked off your fake, 'we never fight' high horse." Thankfully, I don't listen to my first instinct much anymore. (What I actually say in those situations is "All married couples fight; the goal is to learn how to fight fair.")

We enter marriages with false expectations, we choose careers with false expectations, we begin debt management with false expectations, we have kids with false expectations, we have timelines with false expectations, we start diets with false expectations, and we chase dreams with false expectations. It's easy to *start* pursuing a God-sized dream, but you'll need to put together all 4,124 LEGO pieces scattered across the floor if you want to finish strong. You'll have to work through moments that cause you pain, anger, exhaustion, disappointment, fear, and discouragement; you'll need to make the decision to keep going even when everything inside of you wants to give up.

So, on a practical level, managing your expectations means being aware from the very beginning that those difficult moments will come. It means knowing up front that achieving your dream will be hard and will require much sacrifice from you.

It also means you need to plan for those difficult moments. How will you respond when a year goes by and you're still chasing your dream? What about five years? Ten? How will you respond when you start to think seriously about giving up? You have the opportunity to plan out your response now, which is critical—because if you wait until you want to quit to start figuring out how to avoid quitting, you'll never make it. You'll quit. So start determining now how you will respond when giving up feels like the best option.

Managing your expectations also means that pursuing your dream is about way more than that single moment when the dream comes true. There are many details that will need to be worked out, many steps you'll need to take.

For example, I was recently invited to plan a trip to Switzerland. My spiritual hero, Gordon MacDonald, invited me to join him on a hiking trip in the Swiss Alps, which sounded amazing. When I first got the invitation, all I wanted to do was talk with Gordon about all the cool things we'd see and how amazing it would be to literally stand at the top of the world. But

Gordon, who knows a lot about finishing strong, kept remind-ing me about the details—what clothes to bring, what kind of shoes to pack, how much money I'd need, and so on.

In other words, Gordon was focused on the steps we'd need to take before we got anywhere close to the top of the mountain. And that's critical, because if we had ignored those steps and just said, "We're going hiking!" we would never have reached the summit. He helped me count the cost.

In the same way, count the cost for your God-sized dream by managing your expectations. Focus on what you need to do now, tomorrow, and a year from now so that you'll have every opportunity to realize that dream and finish strong.

FIGHT BACK AGAINST DISCOURAGEMENT

Just as every married couple fights, all people experience dis-couragement. There's no pill you can take every morning to protect yourself against it. Discouragement will come.

We discussed earlier how discouragement is especially common for those of us chasing a God-sized dream. Why is that? Because there's usually a big gap between starting to pur-sue a dream and actually achieving it.

We feel overwhelmed when, even after praying for something over the course of years, there seems to be no change—when your marriage still feels as though it's break-ing to pieces, when you're still battling that addiction, when you have the same financial fears month after month, or when it feels as if your cherished and longed-for future will never come to pass.

Jesus Himself warned us of hardship when He said, "Here on earth you will have many trials and sorrows. But take heart, because I have overcome the world" (John 16:33).

Discouragement is constantly knocking at the door of those who pray bold prayers, dream big dreams, and believe that they were born for big things. But that's not always bad news. Think of it this way: discouragement is the emotional evidence that what you're fighting for is worth the fight. It's a logical consequence to any serious dream. I've never gotten discouraged over something that meant nothing to me.

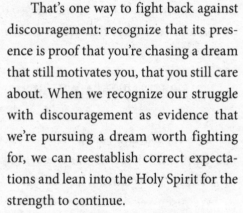

DISCOURAGEMENT IS THE EMOTIONAL EVIDENCE THAT WHAT YOU'RE FIGHTING FOR IS WORTH THE FIGHT.

That's one way to fight back against discouragement: recognize that its presence is proof that you're chasing a dream that still motivates you, that you still care about. When we recognize our struggle with discouragement as evidence that we're pursuing a dream worth fighting for, we can reestablish correct expectations and lean into the Holy Spirit for the strength to continue.

Here are some other helpful ways to fight back against discouragement:

Consult

One of the great things about having heroes in your life is that you can consult with them when times are tough. You can talk with people who've gone before you and probably experienced what you're experiencing in that moment.

The Bible says, "Share each other's burdens, and in this way obey the law of Christ" (Gal. 6:2). Notice that's a two-way street. It's great to have people who are willing to help us carry our burdens, including the burden of discouragement. But in order for that to happen, we need to be willing to share. We need to open up and be vulnerable with those we trust.

Notice also that we need to have others participating in our lives. This is not a biblical suggestion; it's a biblical command. Isolation often leads to elimination when it comes to our spiritual lives—and to our God-given dreams.

I'm thankful I have some incredible heroes in my life—men and women I look up to immensely who have invested themselves in my dreams. They are my go-to resources when I'm feeling discouraged about the challenges that come with pursuing my God-sized dreams.

Capture

Another way to fight back against discouragement is to capture negative thoughts. No, this isn't a new age concept. I didn't learn it from Confucius. I learned it from Scripture: "We destroy every proud obstacle that keeps people from knowing God. We capture their rebellious thoughts and teach them to obey Christ" (2 Cor. 10:5).

Did you know you don't have to let your thoughts drive you and control you? Instead, you have the power to capture those thoughts that lead you in a direction contrary to where you desire to go. You can train your thoughts to be obedient to God's Word.

How does it work? When you get hit with discouragement or other negative thoughts, you need to recognize it and reject it. That will sound something like this:

- "No, I reject this thought that I will never find happiness."
- "I reject the lie that my career is stuck and I will not advance."
- "I say no to the lie that I will never find freedom from this addiction. That is not true, and I reject it."

These are short, quick, knife-sharp prayers, and I recommend saying them out loud when you're able. They are a real way for you to take control of your thoughts rather than allowing your thoughts to control you.

Control

Not only can you control your thought life by capturing negative thoughts, you can also take the reins of your mind by actively declaring positive words and positive truths over your life. Again, this is a biblical concept: "The tongue can bring death or life" (Prov. 18:21). Jesus said, "The words you say will either acquit you or condemn you" (Matt. 12:37).

Again, I recommend that you declare these statements out loud, which might sound like this:

- "I am a child of God, and He cares for me. He will bring me the desires of my heart."
- "God is the provider for my family, and I trust Him with my career."
- "I have been healed of my sin by the blood of Jesus that was shed on the cross, and I will gain victory over this addiction."

Remember, your tongue has the power of life and death. So choose to speak life.

In fact, why not give it a try right now? If you are dealing with poisonous thoughts, or if there are negative ideas that often recur in your mind, take a moment to reject them. Right where you are at this minute, declare them to be lies and say no to them retaining any power over your mind. Then, replace those negative thoughts by declaring what you know to be true about yourself, your God, and your future.

Commit

Finally, when discouragement is trying to knock you off course from pursuing your dreams, make a fresh commitment to trust God's promises.

Here's an example: "We know that God causes everything to work together for the good of those who love God and are called according to his purpose for them" (Rom. 8:28). That's a promise from God to you. That's something you can count on, and it's a truth you can commit to believing.

God has also promised that you are His child and that He cares for you. That you are His masterpiece. He's promised that no weapon formed against you will prosper and that He will empower you to such a degree that problems that feel like mountains crushing down on you can be picked up and tossed into the sea.

Don't let discouragement knock you off course. In the gap between where you are and where your dreams are realized, surround yourself with wisdom, think with purpose, speak truth, and declare the promises of God over your life. We will all face discouragement, but we don't have to lose the battle against it. Choose to fight back and keep moving forward toward your dreams and your hopes for tomorrow!

FOCUS ON WHAT YOU CAN CONTROL

Jennifer and I recently overhauled our entire backyard. In the process, we had to replace the loam and plant new grass. My friend Scott owns a landscaping company and offered to hydroseed my lawn for me.

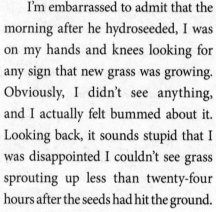

SURROUND YOURSELF WITH WISDOM, THINK WITH PURPOSE, SPEAK TRUTH, AND DECLARE THE PROMISES OF GOD OVER YOUR LIFE.

I'm embarrassed to admit that the morning after he hydroseeded, I was on my hands and knees looking for any sign that new grass was growing. Obviously, I didn't see anything, and I actually felt bummed about it. Looking back, it sounds stupid that I was disappointed I couldn't see grass sprouting up less than twenty-four hours after the seeds had hit the ground.

Why was I disappointed? Because I was focusing on a goal that was unrealistic and outside my control.

Thankfully, I redirected my attention toward what I *could* do. For the next two weeks, I faithfully watered my lawn according to Scott's instructions. I controlled what I could control, and it wasn't long before I was riding my lawn-mower over a beautiful new lawn. In that moment, I didn't need to understand the science behind getting grass to grow;

I just needed to remain committed to the process. When I simply did my part and watered the lawn according to the proper schedule, the grass grew into exactly what it was always intended to become.

Here's the point: we will exhaust ourselves in the pursuit of our dreams if we keep trying to manage things over which we have no control. Remember, God is the one who ultimately empowers us to achieve our God-sized dreams. We have a role to play and we have a lot of work to do, but we'll only drive ourselves to discouragement if we try to do God's job for Him. Instead, we need to focus on what we can control.

I've encountered this same principle in every area of my life. When it comes to pastoring Next Level Church, I frequently need to remind myself, "Josh, focus on what you can control." When it comes to unanswered prayer: "Josh, focus on what you can control." When I'm staring at a meat-lover's pizza while trying to lose weight: "Josh, focus on what you can control."

In what ways are you trying to do God's job for Him right now? As you start building momentum in this process of chasing your dreams, what are the things that only God can accomplish—and how are you wearing yourself out trying to accomplish them on your own?

If you have a dream for financial freedom, for example, there will be lots of things outside of your control. The national economy and the stock market are pretty big examples. So are the whims of bankers and the decisions by the higher-ups in your company. However, none of those things are outside of God's control. There are many things you *can* control as you chase that dream—get yourself on a budget, work to pay off debt, invest wisely, make your case for promotions and raises, and so on. Focus on those and let God do what only He can do.

Now, you may be thinking about all the times when you gave your very best, took care of everything within your control, and things *still* didn't go how you hoped. Trust me, I've been there. But let me ask you this: Who determines the timeline of your dream?

If you had never witnessed anyone else's dreams come true, would you be so discouraged by the fact that yours hasn't come true yet? Would you be more likely to continue your pursuit of that dream if you didn't have other stories to compare yours against? Perhaps if we could never see our neighbors' lawns, we would find more joy and remain more faithful in watering our own.

> YOUR TIMING AND GOD'S TIMING MAY NOT BE THE SAME, BUT THAT DOESN'T MEAN GOD ISN'T STILL RIGHT THERE WITH YOU ON THE JOURNEY.

Your timing and God's timing may not be the same, but that doesn't mean God isn't still right there with you on the journey. Don't allow your past experience or the experiences of others to plunge you into discouragement.

The apostle Paul referred to the Christian journey as a race. In Philippians 3:12–14, he wrote:

> I don't mean to say that I have already achieved these things or that I have already reached perfection. But I press on to possess that perfection for which Christ Jesus first possessed me. No, dear brothers and sisters, I have not

achieved it, but I focus on this one thing: Forgetting the past and looking forward to what lies ahead, I press on to reach the end of the race and receive the heavenly prize for which God, through Christ Jesus, is calling us.

Did you catch that? Paul said that he focused on one thing to help him finish strong: "Forgetting the past and looking forward to what lies ahead." We need to follow his instructions to forget what's already happened and focus on what we can accomplish today. We must focus only on what we can control.

There's one more thing I need to say on this subject, and it's important: sometimes our dreams really do end in a way that's outside of our control. There will be times when you are putting in the work and controlling only what you can control, and God still closes the door. Sometimes He does allow a dream to die.

And that's okay.

Because no one dream defines who you are or what you will accomplish with your future. God does. And when He allows a dream to die, you can trust He has a new dream ready to be birthed in your heart.

For those reasons, sometimes finishing strong means choosing to find peace when God closes the door on the future you wanted, and then choosing to trust Him and pursue the new dream He is about to set in front of you.

I don't know what chapter of your story you're in today. I don't know where your journey began, and I don't know how you ended up where you are right now. I don't know what God's dream is for you, and I don't know how severely stacked against you the odds may feel at this very moment.

The one thing I do know with absolute certainty is that you can do this. Through the power of Christ, you can finish strong. It's not too late. In fact, it's never too late!

IT'S NEVER TOO LATE

When we started this journey together, I told you about my favorite ride at Disney World, the Carousel of Progress. In the early 1920s, when Walt Disney started his first animation studio, he had no idea about the many setbacks and failures he'd experience on his road to success.

In 1923, Walt's dream hit its first wall when he didn't have the revenue needed to keep his studio, Iwerks-Disney Commercial Artists, afloat. In fact, he was forced to close up shop after just a month. At that point, he could have used discouragement as an excuse to give up. Instead, he moved forward, and a short time later, he began another animation business called Laugh-O-gram.

Not long after opening that business, Walt was buying meals on credit from the restaurant downstairs. Then he resorted to eating canned beans alone in his office at night when even the restaurant wouldn't help him any longer. After trying every possible means to borrow more money, Walt resigned himself to bankruptcy and failure number two. In less than five years, Walt Disney, one of the greatest creative minds of the twentieth century, started and closed his first two attempts at his dream.

At that point, Walt Disney had a choice to make. And it's the same choice you and I must make every day: *Do I give up, or do I choose to believe that anything is possible?*

Walt chose to stay positive and look ahead, but because of his two business failures, he couldn't find a bank or investor willing to give him another shot. With nowhere else to turn, Walt traveled to Hollywood to partner with his brother Roy and asked other family members to invest in his dream. When his uncle George agreed to provide the seed money for Disney Brothers Cartoon Studio, little did he know that he'd just invested in something that would touch the lives of billions of people.[2]

There were other ups and downs. Walt created Mickey Mouse in 1928, and his short films quickly gained favor with movie audiences. But then Walt ran out of money again shortly before completing his first major animated film, *Snow White and the Seven Dwarfs*, so he had to talk a bank into loaning him enough capital to keep things afloat. *Snow White* was a major success in 1937, but Disney's next films all flopped at the box office for years. Again and again, Walt found himself with his back against the wall.

In one of his most challenging moments, he wrote these words to a close friend: "The entire situation is a catastrophe. The spirit that played such an important part of the cartoon medium has been destroyed. I have a case of the DDs—disillusionment and discouragement."[3]

Time and again, Disney ran into hardships as he chased his dreams. Over and over, he faced the temptation to settle for a less hopeful future. But he kept going. At one point, Disney said, "I have had a stubborn, blind confidence in the cartoon medium, a determination to show the skeptics that the animated cartoon was deserving of a better place."[4]

Walt could have given up several times when his dream

appeared dead, but his "stubborn, blind confidence" in the dream in his heart kept him moving forward. He risked failure dozens of times—often being told he was crazy or stupid by both detractors and friends—because he understood that endurance is required to finish strong.

Today, our culture celebrates the perfectly posed photos taken when someone crosses the finish line of an important race, but we often ignore the sweaty, painful miles of endurance, grit, faith, and hard work it takes to reach the end. Dreams are freely given away but not freely achieved. They always come with the constant companions of disillusionment and discouragement—yet those who are willing to endure the pain are more likely to achieve their dreams.

God has a great, big, beautiful tomorrow in store for you. He has a plan and purpose for your life. You may think your best days are behind you. You may want to give up chasing your dreams because you've prayed for years, pursued for years, and it seems easier to let things die than to live another day without the hope of those dreams coming true. If so, let me remind you of the words Jesus spoke to Lazarus: "Remove the graveclothes."

You have not been placed on this earth just to breathe, survive, or limp through life injured by yesterday's disappointments. God wants you to thrive! To live as if the same Spirit that raised Jesus from the dead lives in you, because He does. It's time to take off the graveclothes, pray with boldness, believe with confidence, let go of yesterday's failures, shake off the opinions of others, and pursue your great, big, beautiful tomorrow.

May you always remember that as long as you have breath in your lungs, a God-sized dream in your heart, and the willingness to finish strong, it's not over!

FINISHING STRONG
IS NOT THE ACT OF
COMPLETING SOMETHING
BUT THE PROCESS WE
GO THROUGH ON OUR
WAY TO COMPLETION.

AFTERWORD

A few days ago, I spent the better part of a morning reading a draft of this soon-to-be-published book, Josh Gagnon's *It's Not Over*. When I reached the last page, I put the manuscript down, mused upon what I'd been reading, and said to myself (out loud), "Self . . . this book is going to provoke a lot of people."

If I were to expand on this conclusion (and I will), I would say that this book is going to provoke a lot of leaders to search their hearts and listen again *for the first time* to what God wants to say to them about these days in which we live and what plans He has to reignite his church with power and spiritual performance.

I have employed the word *provoke* because that is what Josh Gagnon did to me. He clearly provoked *me* (in the best possible way) to do some of that thinking about my days as an influencer (if I actually am one) and what new initiatives God might have in store for me in the waning years of my life.

So how has Josh's book provoked me? Is it the way that the author became transparent as he used himself—his story, his aspirations, his strengths, and his weaknesses—to give the reader a picture of what's possible when God anoints leaders and generates God-sized (the author's term) dreams? Or was I provoked by his many useful references to biblical personalities and the principles by which they, in God's strength, led nations, churches, and kingdom-centered expeditions?

Or was there something else in the reading that had reached deep into my heart? Something I had yet to fully pin down?

Later in the day of my first reading of *It's Not Over*, I picked up Josh's manuscript again and scanned the pages I'd marked up earlier. This time, something suddenly became clearer to me. While reading the book, I had begun to regain a picture of myself as I once was in my youngish years when I, like the author, was dealing with those challenges and imaginations that can come alive when one is called upon to offer a bit of leadership in the Christian movement.

I hope it will not offend my friend Josh if I say that I realized I used to be a lot like him. I, too, was once a visionary pastor, similarly brave in my willingness to take risks if I believed God was pushing or pulling me (wherever He wishes to be).

It's not that I have abandoned or discarded such a spirit of excitability concerning God's purposes. Rather, it's that I've now reached an age—old enough to be the author's father—where the time has come to step a bit to the side, stop running churches and organizations, and cheer on (*mentor* is an appropriate word) another generation of men and women like Josh who are hearing God's voice in fresh, new ways.

Now, take those God-sized dreams Josh shares with the reader as he tells the story of the founding of the Next Level Church and its ever-enlarging network of congregations. Many of us have *been there, done that* as we, too, once responded to the nudges of God's call. But I must admit that we didn't do it in as unstable a time as Josh and his colleagues do it today. Today, there's a need for an audacity, a leap-off-the-cliff mentality that those of us in my generation didn't need quite so badly.

What Josh and his people (and others) are willing to do today to test God's faithfulness utterly amazes me. It charms me into admiration for them.

As I brooded on portions of *It's Not Over* a second and a third time, I was reminded of mornings when I, too, used to awaken with faith-driven ideas I could not wait to share with the people in my world. Usually, the first one to hear about one of my new innovations was my wife, Gail, who often marveled at how fast my mind could race when a new inspiration exploded into life in my heart. Too often she felt the need to lower my temperature with one paralyzing question: "Honey, how much do you think that will cost?"

Then there were my pastoral staff associates, who learned to brace themselves when I requested an extra staff meeting that hadn't been on the office calendar. It was usually a sign that something new was up. And finally, there was the congregation that figured out it had managed to call a pastor who always had a great plan for their lives (and their energies and their money).

In those days I was sort of a mad scientist, ready to try anything. At least that's my perception of myself—and of Josh Gagnon. (I say this with respect and a smile.)

In *It's Not Over*, Josh has written about his life of imaginings, about casting larger-than-life visions. His greatest of all visions? Next Level Church, which boasts locations (like Starbucks) all the way from Quebec to Florida.

This is no small church-planting effort that Josh and his team have accomplished. As he himself says, he didn't launch his ministry as an experienced pastoral leader with an abundance of formal theological training. Rather, he stepped out daringly when he became animated with the passion that people needed to hear the salvation-based story of Jesus Christ and what it means to follow Him. Furthermore, a lot of things fell into place in Josh's perspective when he became convinced that people needed to commit to communities of "saints" (spiritually hungry people), where people of all ages and backgrounds could grow in a Jesus-like way and serve Him purposefully.

Josh Gagnon doesn't pretend to the reader (and this is important) that the life of a dreamer-leader is a simple or easy one. He is candid in admitting that there were for him many experiences of tears, discouragements, outright mistakes, and opposition from people inside and outside the church. Josh fully admits that occasionally the temptation can rise to run from everything. But, obviously, he hasn't caved yet.

But I must go on to say that the theme of this book is not about the gloomy side of leadership. Rather, it is a book focused on telling us what happens when leaders choose to bank on the faithfulness of Jesus' promises.

Josh Gagnon and I both live in New England. We know from experience that our region of North America is one of the most challenging places there is to draw people to Jesus and to challenge them to become part of gatherings that want to make a difference in their communities. If your ability to appreciate the role of faith is weak, then this is not a region to come to.

I have known a time when "knowledgeable" church leaders from our part of the world would have watched Josh and others like him do what they do and muttered to one another, "This will never work in New England."

But, in fact, it has. And Josh has provided us with a picture of what doing things in New England can look like, if you have faith, a willingness to work hard, a great vision, and a loyal team. And also a picture of a God who is behind it all.

In the last chapters of *It's Not Over*, Josh Gagnon has addressed himself to the place of the Spirit of God and his empowerment to all who seek the bold life of the Christ follower. It's this theme of empowerment that binds the entire book together and makes it more than just a book of tales and techniques. This is the part of the book where Josh makes it clear to all of us—the younger and the older—that the Christian brand of leadership depends wholly on the way we draw God's Spirit into the center of our vision and dreams. I am much appreciative of Josh's humility as he traces for the reader the centrality of the Spirit of God and his willingness to take common, ordinary people and make them into champions.

And so I return to my opening comment: that this book has provoked me. To what? To the fresh assurance that nothing is impossible when a young leader (when *any* leader) hears God's call, renounces the forces of fear and doubt, and starts each day with a fresh anticipation that God is going to do something unusual and life-changing. Under such influence, one can say with confidence: *it's not over*. It never has been over in the past. It isn't now. And it certainly won't be over in the days to come.

When Josh Gagnon calls me or writes an email to me, he almost always ends the written or spoken communication with these words: "Love you, Pastor." And so I close this writing in a similar way: "Love you, too, Josh. Thanks for provoking us."

—Gordon MacDonald
Concord, New Hampshire

ACKNOWLEDGMENTS

It's impossible to ever see a dream as big as a book come true without being surrounded by an amazing group of people who encourage you not only in the process of writing but in all the years preceding putting the first words on a page.

First and foremost, thank you to Jennifer, Malachi, and Nehemiah. You are and always will be my most important legacy. Thank you for all your support in this process. We wrote this book together! I love you.

Mom, Dad, and Matthew: Can you believe your son/ brother who couldn't pass English class in high school wrote a book? Well, believe it! Thank you all for loving me and shaping me into the man I am today.

Roman, Michelle, Walter, Maegan, Daniel, and Katherine: Thank you for believing in me when I didn't even believe in myself. Thank you for chasing this God-sized dream with me. I love you!

To my literary agent, Alex Field: This book never would've happened without you. Thank you for continually speaking life into this dream!

To Megan Dobson, Meaghan Porter, and the amazing team at W: You've been awesome to work with! Thank you for believing in me and making me a better writer. I can't wait to do this again.

To Sam O'Neal and George Dupree: Thank you for your contributions. This book wouldn't be what it is without you.

To Brad Lomenick: Thank you for telling me for years that I needed to write and for being the one God used to open this door.

To the staff of Next Level Church: We are living proof that dreams come true! Every one of you means so much to me, and you each have your fingerprints in these pages.

To the wonderful people of NLC: Thank you for being a church that is willing to chase big dreams. It is such an honor to be your pastor. The best is ahead!

To Gordon and Gail MacDonald: Thank you for being heroes in the lives of Jen and me. We've been able to point our arrows in a more purposeful direction because of your wisdom in our lives.

To the One who first placed this dream in me: Thank You for equipping and calling me and for giving me the joy of serving You. I pray that this book brings You glory.

NOTES

Introduction: A Great, Big, Beautiful Tomorrow

1. Nina Zipkin, "16 Inspirational Quotes from Walt Disney," Entrepreneur.com, December 15, 2016, https://www.entrepreneur .com/article/286080.

Chapter 1: Sweet Dreams Are Made of This

1. D. L. Moody, *Power from On High* (London: Morgan and Scott, 1882), 48.
2. William Whitworth, "Kentucky-Fried," *New Yorker*, February 6, 1970, https://www.newyorker.com/magazine/1970/02/14 /kentucky-fried.
3. Venessa Wong, "Everything You Don't Know About the Real Colonel Sanders," Buzzfeed News, July 9, 2015, https://www .buzzfeednews.com/article/venessawong/the-real-colonel -sanders.

Chapter 2: Life on a Stump

1. James Bennet, "Mandela, at White House, Says World Backs Clinton," *New York Times*, September 23, 1998, A26.
2. *Merriam-Webster*, s.v. "disappointing," accessed September 23, 2019, https://www.merriam-webster.com/dictionary /disappointing.
3. Kavod v'Nichum and Gamliel Institute, "Shemira," accessed September 23, 2019, https://www.jewish-funerals.org/shemira/.

Chapter 3: Sawzall the Wall

1. C. S. Lewis, *Surprised by Joy* (London: Harcourt Brace & Company), 160.

Chapter 4: Predictable Resistance

1. Steven Pressfield, *The War of Art* (Black Irish Entertainment LLC, 2002), https://books.google.com/books?id=sR3hAAAAQBAJ &printsec=frontcover&dq=Pressfied+The+Art+of+War&hl =en&sa=X&ved=2ahUKEwi25snLja3kAhUFi6wKHX4Y CkcQ6AEwAHoECAQQAg#v=snippet&q=two%20lives&f =false.

2. Chris Woodford, "Airplanes," ExplainThatStuff.com, June 16, 2019, https://www.explainthatstuff.com/howplaneswork.html.

Chapter 5: When Life Hands You 4,124 LEGOs

1. Larry Chang, *Wisdom for the Soul* (Washington, DC: Gnosophia Publishers, 2006), 233.

Chapter 6: Enemies, Encouragers, and Experts—Oh My!

1. "*Rudy* Turns 25! The Film's Most Memorable Quotes," *Parade*, October 13, 2018, https://parade.com/708397/solanahawkenson /rudy-turns-25-the-films-most-memorable-quotes/.

2. Michael Foust, "TNT's Ernie Johnson in Viral Comments: 'I'm Going to Pray for Donald Trump,'" *Christian Examiner*, November 10, 2016, https://www.christianexaminer.com /article/tnts-ernie-johnson-in-viral-comments-im-going-to -pray-for-donald-trump/51215.htm.

Chapter 7: Dangerous Prayers

1. "18 Martin Luther Quotes That Still Ring True," *Relevant*, October 31, 2017, https://relevantmagazine.com/god/15 -martin-luther-quotes-still-ring-true/.

2. "History," SpaffordCenter.org, http://www.spaffordcenter.org /history.

Chapter 8: What's So Scary About the Holy Spirit?

1. Oswald Chambers, *Biblical Psychology* (Grand Rapids, MI: Discovery House, 1995), chapter 17.

Chapter 9: Finish Strong

1. Ravi Zacharias, *I, Isaac, Take Thee, Rebekah: Moving from Romance to Lasting Love* (Nashville: Thomas Nelson, 2005), 25.
2. Bob Thomas, *Walt Disney: An American Original* (New York: Disney Editions, 1976).
3. Steven Watts, *The Magic Kingdom: Walt Disney and the American Way of Life* (Columbia, MO: University of Missouri Press, 1997), 228.
4. Michael Barrier, *The Animated Man: A Life of Walt Disney* (University of California Press, 2007), 4.

ABOUT THE AUTHOR

Joshua Gagnon is the founding and lead pastor of Next Level Church, which is regularly recognized as one of the fastest growing churches in America. He is known for his uniquely authentic communication style that makes the hope found in Jesus relevant to people of every background. He and his wife, Jennifer, raise their two sons in New Hampshire.